Making a Difference
Stories from the Point of Care
Volume I

BOOKS OF STORIES BY AND ABOUT NURSES

From the Honor Society of Nursing, Sigma Theta Tau International

---

A Daybook for Nurses: Making a Difference Each Day, Hudacek, 2004.

Making a Difference: Stories from the Point of Care, Volume I, Hudacek, 2005.

Making a Difference: Stories from the Point of Care, Volume II, Hudacek, 2004.

Pivotal Moments in Nursing: Leaders Who Changed the Path of a Profession, Houser and Player, 2004.

Ordinary People, Extraordinary Lives: The Stories of Nurses, Smeltzer and Vlasses, 2003.

The HeART of Nursing: Expressions of Creative Art in Nursing, Wendler, 2002.

Stories of Family Caregiving: Reconsideration of Theory, Literature, and Life, Poirier and Ayres, 2002.

As We See Ourselves: Jewish Women in Nursing, Benson, 2001.

Cadet Nurse Stories: The Call for and Response of Women During World War II, Perry and Robinson, 2001.

The Adventurous Years: Leaders in Action 1973-1999, Watts, 1998.

For more information and to order these and other books from the Honor Society of Nursing, Sigma Theta Tau International, visit **www.nursingsociety.org/publications**; or go to **www.nursingknowledge.org/stti/books**, the Web site of Nursing Knowledge International, the honor society's sales and distribution division; or call 1.888.NKI.4.YOU (U.S. and Canada) or +1.317.634.8171 (outside U.S. and Canada).

Making a Difference
Stories from the Point of Care
Volume I

Sharon Hudacek, RN, EdD

Sigma Theta Tau International
Honor Society of Nursing

Indianapolis, Indiana, USA

Sigma Theta Tau International

Editor-in-Chief: Jeff Burnham

Acquisitions Editor: Fay L. Bower, RN, DNSc, FAAN

Project Editor: Carla Hall

Copy Editor: Estelle Beaumont, RN, PhD

Proofreader: Linda Canter

Cover Design: Gary Adair

Composition and Interior Design: Rebecca Harmon

Printed in the United States of America

Printing and Binding by V.G. Reed & Sons

Sigma Theta Tau International

550 West North Street

Indianapolis, IN 46202

Visit our Web site at www.nursingsociety.org/stti/books for more information on our books and other publications.

ISBN: 1-930538-15-4

Library of Congress Cataloging-in-Publication Data: Available upon request

05 06 07 08 / 9 8 7 6 5 4 3 2 1

Table of Contents at a Glance

Table of Contents

Acknowledgments

A project of this magnitude could not have been possible without the assistance and work ethic of some very key people. Initially a research study, and now a book, this work requires special thanks and recognition to:

My research assistants and nurse practitioner colleagues, Mary Triano, Karen Robson, and Mary Walsh who were always there to collect data, sort it, and learn about phenomenology. To Jodi Quintavalle and Janice Varneke, my undergraduate research assistants.

Faculty and administrators at the University of Scranton—an incredible learning environment. I have been a faculty member for 10 years and each year I have been more amazed at the generous support for faculty goals and dreams.

Drs. Pat Harrington, and Georgia Narsavage, for their support and friendship. To my best friend, Dr. Dona Carpenter, who took many of the photographs for this book. She is always there for me.

Drs. Mary Muscari, RN, and Lee Ann Eschbach, at the University of Scranton, who saw the value in this study and helped me to "get the project off the ground." Kevan Bailey and Ray Burd made sure the printouts and mailings were always in order. Dr. Helen Streubert kept the research method on track, read through the stories, and identified themes and unifying data.

Dr. Mary Aukerman and Leon Green at the University of Pittsburgh were entirely supportive. Dr. Linda Scaz, a leader, friend, and advocate for hospice patients. Mary Hale and the other pediatric nurses in Philadelphia, whose writings about the "Comfort Basket" made me incredibly grateful for what nurses do when caring for the little ones.

All the organizations who were so helpful in notifying prospective contributors.

Maude Smith, who was a mentor and pen pal at the time I needed it most!

All of the contributing authors who gave their time and told beautiful, caring accounts about special patients. You made this book possible and I respect your work. I hope this book continues to lift your spirits and is both pleasing to you and challenging as you continue your excellent work. It is what you do that makes life better for the patients and families in your care.

Judy Burns, my friend who edited the manuscript before its journey to Sigma Theta Tau International. Your talent, experience, and the giving of your time were all vital to this project. You provided the balance of care and humor that helped me finish.

The nurses at Mercy and Moses Taylor Hospital, Scranton, Pennsylvania, USA, for assisting with the pictures in this book.

My parents, Kay and Charles Smith, who—thank God—are always there for me, and my sister, Dr. Deb Mileski, for her upbeat nature, the psychologist's forte.

Paul Branks for repeatedly discussing with me the need to get this book published through Sigma Theta Tau International. Dr. Estelle Beaumont, the copy editor who contributed enormous time and talent to the project. Dr. Lynda Carpenito, who reviewed the manuscript, helped to improve the quality, and assured me that the work was valid and important to our profession. Martha Rogers, who guided me on the "Soul of Nursing." Sue MacDonald, whose editing and suggestions were so important. I am most grateful to my "west coast mentor," Fay Bower. Fay's energy, expertise, and guidance came at a time when this manuscript needed her! I am so appreciative of her wisdom, style, and experience.

Stephen and Chas, my young sons who got very used to the fax and scanner—and never questioned my need to work long hours, or sift through stacks of mail at their basketball games.

My husband, Steve, who has read every story and told me from the first that I had a mission and commitment to the nurses who contributed—to publish this work. He encouraged me and was my best friend and driving force. He read—and read—and cried, intrigued by the beauty of the nurses' stories.

Author's Note

Five years ago, the first volume of *Making a Difference: Stories from the Point of Care* was written. It was a time of great inquiry into the work of nurses—the everyday work of everyday nurses. During the 1990s, the nursing profession learned a great deal about itself. Through studies like the Woodhull Study of Nursing Practice, nurses came to realize that their work was not recognized in mainstream media and that nurses were largely behind the scenes. Silent, humble, dedicated nurses, the glue to any healthcare organization, were all too frequently not noticed.

Imagine the talent of the millions of nurses in the United States and around the world. Imagine the sadness in not telling or knowing their stories? The stories of nurses have been in captivity for years because, I believe, few have asked.

The book *Making a Difference* changed nursing in a big way. In May of 2000, the first volume of *Making a Difference: Stories from the Point of Care* was published to give voice to talented nurses who made a difference in the lives of patients and families. *Making a Difference* gave nurses time to tell the story. *Making a Difference* listened to nurses. *Making a Difference* gave nurses credit for their work and validated dedication. It was a book that highlighted special moments etched in the memories of nurses. It gave nurses permission and encouraged them to full-heartedly journal and reflect on some very difficult-but-critical times in their lives. While painful, many of the stories brought a sense of joy to the tellers, long past the event. Nurses remembered when their actions saved a life, or made life a little better for someone else. Nurses documented history and a legacy for future nurses by relating each account.

The words of nurses are powerful indeed. Many nurses feel an inner strength and spiritual connection as they write their stories. These stories tell a tale; they are poetry in action. The inner drive and love for the profession shines through in each word.

Tears, joy, and other emotions are vital reasons to write. Transforming feelings into written narratives is healing. Nursing is a profession filled with sorrow and question. I truly believe that telling the story heals the nurse's soul.

Each story adds to a scrapbook of caring. Each story is built on wisdom, experience, and tremendous dedication. The words and stories of nurses describe vivid memoirs of the human experience of caring. The stories are persuasive and intense. The stories reveal the magnitude of caring and a love for humanity.

In this expanded and revised edition of *Making A Difference: Stories from the Point of Care, Volume I,* I am allowed to reflect on the goodness and importance of my research. My phenomenological research focuses on the stories of nurses—stories that occur in the mundane, tragic, joyful, or even mysterious cadence of the human journey. These stories, recounted by nurses, are reflections of deeply meaningful relationships shared with patients.

For the past 10 years, my research has allowed me to collect and publish the stories of nurses. This has been my greatest commitment—to honor other nurses by making their words known. To give nurses a voice; to listen and hear them. It is the right thing to do, and I thank Sigma Theta Tau International for allowing me to do it.

Making a Difference Volume I allowed me to help others. In 2002, I began the Making A Difference in Nursing Foundation, a scholarship fund to assist LPN nurses to return to school for a bachelor's degree in nursing. All book royalties go to this foundation that is housed at the

University of Scranton. Each year, at least one LPN is given a scholarship to support his or her education. Truly, this foundation has given me tremendous satisfaction in helping other nurses advance their educational pathways. The purpose of our profession is to care for others. The strength of our profession, I believe, lies within helping each other.

Making a Difference, Volume II, published in December 2004 has allowed me to continue to write for nurses. Now, over 220 stories written by incredible nurses have been published in the two volumes of *Making a Difference.* Over 210 quotes from nurses are now printed in *A Daybook for Nurses; Making A Difference Everyday,* published in November 2004. Slowly but surely, the many beautiful and varied voices of nurses are being heard.

The *Making A Difference* series of books (Volume I, Volume II, and the Daybook) tells you simply and honestly what nurses do. By reading the stories of nurses, the reader gets an inside look at the greatness in the profession, the diversity, the giving, and the thinking. One doesn't have to be a nurse to appreciate the pages within. All of us have been touched by a nurse, but none of us can appreciate the magnitude of caring unless we carefully read, page by page, the stories.

I have always been so proud to be a nurse. What I haven't been proud of is the lack of recognition nurses receive; in the media, in healthcare, and in academia. Even in the midst of an international nursing shortage, few nurses are asked their opinions or advice when, in fact, they are often the best resource. Little is known about their work. Few really understand what it takes to be a nurse and the commitment of these healthcare heroes. The lack of nurses on national news and in the media continues to be an enormous problem.

I am trying to change that. *Making A Difference* is changing that. Like never before, the work of nurses is in black and white, for all readers. The best-kept secrets about nurses and the tremendous impact they make in the world in which they live are revealed in these *Making a Difference* books.

Thank you for taking the time to read the words of nursing colleagues and enter into the day to day world of extraordinary nurses. Perhaps the next time you meet a nurse somewhere, someplace, sometime, you will take a moment to thank him or her for always being a breath away, should that breath be needed.

Sharon Hudacek, RN, EdD

Preface

It was a cool day in Pittsburgh, Pennsylvania, when nurse leaders gathered. The lively panel discussed the role of nursing and our consistent lack of visibility to the public and media.

Nurses can't always remain behind the scenes. That must change soon. For the work of nurses is celebrated by so few—maybe mostly by colleagues in hallowed hallways of academe or in cluttered breakrooms of hospitals. But nurses are brave and often heroic. Only those who use their hearts and hands to heal and comfort know the true meaning of the work that nurses do. Quiet, peaceful, and satisfied, nurses are the silent workers for humanity.

How It Began

I had quite a different project in mind for my next study, I assure you. I planned to do a very clinical study involving molecular biology—until that day in Pittsburgh when I heard my nurse colleagues talk about nursing work. Call it fate or just being touched by an angel. That is truly how this project began.

I heard Melanie Dreher, then the president of the Honor Society of Nursing, Sigma Theta Tau International, speak about current dilemmas facing nurses all over the country and the need for our profession to get the "good word" out about what we actually do. What an incredibly good thought. As I thought about this challenge I realized, "I can do that. I need to do that. What a wonderful contribution that would be to those I care about—other colleagues in nursing." And the journey began.

Why It Began

For almost 20 years, I have been a practicing nurse and educator. I have a lot of education, but my best education has been working with other nurses on the front lines. The nurses who are out there every day, evening, night, holiday, and weekend—through impossible weather, war zones, bombings—to do what they do best: nurse.

What do you think about when you hear the word "nurse?" Many of you have been cared for by a nurse, know a nurse, or are related to one. It is not difficult to appreciate that person for the ability to care and the knowledge that substantiates that ability to care.

In your family, nurses are usually there at the drop of a hat when someone is sick. They are the first to be called to verify a new drug or diagnosis. They may even be brewing a pot of chicken soup for an aunt who is ill. Nurses are often asked to comment about a specific doctor, recommend a good internist, and give advice about back pain and kidney stones. They answer such questions as these: What is a fibroid? Is CPR something I should take because my dad has heart disease? How do I feed this new baby? Do you think my child has a fever?

In this book, I asked nurses to tell the previously untold. I asked them to "Say what you do." Feel the emotions and write the words. Think about that caring moment that keeps you going—that time in your professional life when you made life or the end of life better for someone. Let people know the heart and soul of nurse work. To that end, their stories were edited only for length and conciseness. The language and style of the storytelling were uncompromised so as to ensure the integrity of their personal accounts. These stories have not been authenticated, but I believe them to be true and genuine.

Every day behind the scenes, nurses are, in fact, courageous. They give so much of themselves. Unfortunately, they often don't tell others—but families and, of course, patients know. As you read these stories, reflect on the magic of nurses' caring.

Introduction

It's 3 a.m. in the Intensive Care Unit. The hallways are quiet, except for the sounds of whirring machines and beeping instruments, breathing life into those who cannot do it alone. Footsteps break the emptiness as the nurse enters each darkened doorway, deliberately checking on every patient. Nurses, the often unseen and unsung health care heroes, enhance technology's miracles with a human touch that, for many, makes the difference between life and death.

Since human civilization began, there have always been people in nursing roles. No communities or societies have ever existed without nurses. Though nursing's roots extend back for centuries, nursing, as we know it today, began in the mid-eighteen hundreds when Florence Nightingale established the first nursing schools and formalized the roles of nurses. For the past hundred and fifty years or so, nursing has evolved just as our society has changed. Nursing's service is, and always has been, to society. It is this ultimate and essential purpose that has been the enduring quality of what many have called the "finest profession."

We find nurses everywhere. They are in our hospitals, clinics, hospices, homes, and schools. They are in nursing homes, homes for the aged, long-term and chronic care institutions. They are in our offices, businesses, sports complexes, and governments. They are working in our homes, in community centers, and in our ghettos. They are in isolated rural outposts, war zones, and catastrophic sites. Soon, they will be in space. Nurses are practitioners, educators, managers, researchers, consultants, policy-makers, entrepreneurs, inventors, politicians, and social advocates. Wherever they are working, regardless of their roles, nurses aim to help people preserve and enhance health, well-being, and quality of life.

Despite the fact that nursing's contribution to the well-being of any society is crucial, as has been demonstrated through decades of health research, the knowledge and work of nurses continues to be under-valued and under-acknowledged. In a time when technology is valued more highly than caring or quality of life, the essential contributions of nursing are partially eclipsed. Although partially eclipsed by present day values and priorities, it is certain that nurses around the world continue to offer themselves in knowledgeable and compassionate care to those in need.

The purpose of this work is to bring into light the work of nurses as they share with people in the sometimes mundane, sometimes tragic, sometimes joyful, and sometimes mysterious cadences of the human journey. The stories, recounted by nurses, are reflections of deeply meaningful relationships shared with patients. Most notably, they are illustrations of the caring spirit. The stories are international, bridging nursing experiences from around the world. From Canada to Sweden, Bosnia to the Slovak Republic and Singapore, nurses reveal a common bond in caring acts administered to their patients.

We are privileged to be able to read the stories contributed by nurses. As thoughtful readers, we can enjoy the simple beauty of each, but we must also look for the deeper meaning embedded in them, both individually and collectively. The spirit of nursing is seen in the ways these nurses are with patients—the actions they take as they give of themselves in the caring-healing mission. But, the actions are also expressions of nurses' knowledge and intellect, of the profoundly moving emotional nature of human relationships and of the very soulful-ness of nursing. The stories are memories in the souls of each of the nurses and are indicative of how nurses are forever affected and changed as a consequence of their relationships with patients.

As the reader will find, many of these stories tell of experiences with dying people. This should not be seen as sad, morose, or depressing. Rather, these are the stories that have poignantly remained in the memories of nurses. They are stories of soulfulness, of how nurses have the honor and privilege of sharing intimately with people during all phases of living and dying. These are powerful stories, but so are those that appear to be simple recollections of the ordinary—the little things. However, to those who are suffering or bearing witness to suffering, the ordinary, little things are anything but ordinary. As many stories reveal, the attention nurses give to the "little things" transforms the ordinary into the extraordinary.

This book is an attempt to give voice to the silent, the humble, the courageous, and the heroic. It is a tribute to the knowledge of nurses and to the capacity of nurses to open their hearts to the feelings of others, no matter how difficult that may be at times. And, it is an opportunity to acknowledge, with reverence, the altruism and passionate commitment of nurses to those in their care. In all, these stories illuminate the fundamental meaning and purpose of nursing—the "finest profession."

CHAPTER 1

Making a Difference: Nurse Work

Nursing reaches back in time to man's beginnings. Nursing is also the kind of work from which all people can benefit. Nurses have cared for and healed the sick all over the world. During many wars, including those in Vietnam and the Persian Gulf, nurses were present and providing care. In natural disasters, nurses reassemble the pieces of shattered lives by providing lifesaving care to the victims of hurricanes and earthquakes. In the chaos of the 1995 Oklahoma City bombing and the 9/11 terrorist attacks on New York City in 2001, nurses were on the scene immediately to aid the injured and comfort those searching for their loved ones. History is replete with the work of nurses.

There's no such thing as a typical workday for a nurse. Sometimes the hospital shift starts at sunrise, but it's just as likely to start at 3 p.m. or 11 p.m. No matter what time the nurse begins work, there's a sense of urgency that starts the work day. It is not unusual for the shift to start something like this:

Cardiac monitors are beeping with the visual display of heart rhythms. There are loud voices, curious aromas, hurried professionals, a burst of laughter, phones ringing, and a fax from the pharmacy. But before the work shift begins, the elevator door opens. A new patient arrives clutching his chest and soaked with perspiration, his reddened face grimacing in pain. A nurse quickly attends to him, strokes his forehead and calmly explains what is happening and reassures him. Two minutes later, the man's eyes roll back as a seizure begins. "Call a Code. I lost his pulse," someone yells above the mayhem. A cart of emergency medications and respiratory supplies is rushed to his bedside. One nurse inserts a needle forcefully into the patient's vein to deliver a drug that calms the fibrillating heart ventricles. Another nurse electrically shocks the chest wall while yet another nurse ensures ventilation. Seconds later, when the cardiac response team arrives, the patient is stabilized. For the rest of the day the admitting nurse spends her time monitoring the patient, frequently checking his vital signs, carefully bathing him, consoling him, teaching him, and answering questions.

✳ *This scenario is just one of the ways nurses make a difference and is an example of nurse work. Nurse work is important, rewarding, and, at times, hard to do. It demands emotional strength and a dedication to helping others. It is constantly changing and diverse and thus requires an incredible amount of knowledge and skill.*

Nurses make decisions that prolong life, save lives, and make lives better. Patients of all ages recover or die in comfort because of what nurses do. At some point, including the very moment of birth, everyone has been cared for by a nurse. Business executives, political advocates, and famous movie stars all have needed the caring service of nurses. In schools, homes, hospices, and sometimes in emergency rooms, people have been touched by the healing hands and caring approach of a nurse.

Only nurses are privileged to intimately enter a patient's life. They help others in ordinary and yet extraordinary ways. Many times it is even heroic. Nurses operate in special ways. Nurses guide, prompt, reinforce decisions, and give and receive strength for spur-of-the moment decisions that might save a life.

HELPING DURING THE DIFFICULT TIMES
by Donna Borer

This story is about a 12-year-old child I'll call Zelda whom I took care of in the ICU where I work. She was diagnosed with a brain tumor and needed surgery. Needless to say she and her family were frightened. The day of surgery I comforted her and her mother as much as possible while trying to explain what would happen. After she went to the operating room, I sat with her mother for a long time, letting her cry and talk. She hugged and thanked me. Zelda returned from surgery awake and crying but intact. However her tumor was malignant, so the prognosis was poor. Before I left that day, the mother thanked me again for caring, and I told her I would take care of Zelda the next morning. As I walked into work the following day, I found Zelda on a ventilator and unresponsive. During the night she had had a grand mal seizure and a respiratory arrest.

My heart sank as I walked into the room and knelt next to Zelda's mother. She hugged me and cried uncontrollably. I could not hold back the tears and cried with her. Two days later I said good-bye to Zelda and her mother. The family had donated her organs for transplant, and Zelda's mother thanked me again, saying she felt I had helped her through a very difficult ordeal.

HELPING WITH STROKE RECOVERY
by Carla Glaus

Several years ago I worked the evening-night shift on a medical unit. One night a young woman patient was admitted with a stroke. She was unable to speak and unable to move her left side. During her hospitalization she was often angry and hostile toward those trying to help her recover. Even though she was older than I was, I somehow felt the pain she was going through and decided I would not give up. I would spend hours with her if only to brush her long hair and talk. As time went on, she began to progress, and eventually it was time to go home. She could now walk with a cane and could speak short phrases. I had become attached to her over the weeks. As I told her good-bye, she took my hand and squeezed it and said, "Thank you" with tears in her eyes. I knew my caring meant something special to her. Everyone needs to feel loved and cared for.

Important work does not always mean the work is extraordinary. It can be as simple as doing little things that make a big difference in the life of the patient. Sometimes it is the little things that patients need most and remember best. It might mean bringing a pet to a dying woman— her only soul mate at the time—or bringing a birthday cake to a pediatric patient. It could also mean a hug, a cup of coffee, and a quick game of cards or a back rub. Perhaps it's comforting hands that hold and heal, or perhaps it's teaching that may one day affect someone's life.

Giving That Last Wish
Martha Debbie Dixon

I met Quentin, an 89-year-old Scottish blind patient, while working the night shift at a county nursing home. Since Quentin could not see with his deep brown eyes, he was not ruled by a clock to strict routines. Around 1:00 a.m. he would pull out his harmonica and start to play hymns, such as "How Great Thou Art" or "Rock of Ages." I would go in to listen and sing along during my rounds. As the months went on, Quentin's body became filled with fluid.

I asked him, "If you could have anything or do anything in this world, what would it be?" He replied, "One more time, before I die, I want to feel the grass under my feet." I told my co-workers I was taking my break. I got Quentin dressed and then took off my shoes and stockings. I would be his eyes on this quest, but we would physically share this experience together. Slowly we made our way down the dimmed hallways, through the sunporch and down onto the wheelchair ramp. Soon our bare feet touched the expanse of grass that was the front lawn to the home. It was 3 a.m. by then on a warm summer night. The phlox were blooming along a stone wall. I guided Quentin there to rest and breathe in the delicate fragrance of the flowers. As we sat there, I asked him, "How does the grass feel Quentin?"

"Soft and moist with dew and oh, so good," he responded. "I'm almost in heaven."

EFFECTIVELY PROMOTING HEALTH IN MEXICO
by Christy M. Spaulding

We worked in a village called Tekit. For clinical, we all dressed in white scrubs. When we arrived at the village, passers-by watched us closely. To have healthcare workers in their village was a big event. We were welcomed to the village by the mayor and were asked to sign our names in the village records book.

In the center of the village was a park surrounded by a Catholic church, the city offices, and other shops made of concrete. Further up the street was an open market where vegetables, meat, clothing, and miscellaneous items were sold. Further away from the village square, on the side streets, we saw older women scrubbing on washboards behind small thatched huts or concrete compounds. Each hut had several hammocks. Children, dressed in rags, played on the dirt roads.

I often felt like I was stepping inside a National Geographic magazine as I walked past those homes. I realized that knowledge could enable them to lengthen their life span and prevent devastating injury or illness. In an effort to help these people with health promotion and prevention, we administered surveys, taught health promotion in the schools, and helped screen people at the small clinic located in the village.

I felt one of the most effective ways to teach health promotion was by educating grade school children about hand washing and dental hygiene. We went to several different schools and brought soap, toothbrushes, and toothpaste samples to pass out to the children. I was in the group that taught dental hygiene. Using homemade models of teeth and a toothbrush, we taught the children how and when to brush their teeth. It was so fun to see the excitement on their faces as we handed them their own personal toothbrush. It was our hope they would take it home and teach their family, or at least establish a personal habit of brushing their own teeth. Even though it seems like such a simple principle, we knew with persistence and by forming that daily habit, these children could be healthier.

I often wondered how effective our few days in Tekit were in promoting health and preventing illness. Our desire to teach the people of Tekit was great. But, without consistent reinforcement, knowledge of the need for change, a desire to change, and resources, the effect of our project on health promotion was most likely minimal. This experience caused me to wonder how we could make health promotion more effective. In order to increase effectiveness, we must collaborate with other disciplines, become better health educators, and base our health promotion measures on sound evidence.

Health promotion must be a collaborative effort among schoolteachers, nurses, governments, companies, and families. By involving people from a variety of disciplines, health promotion is reinforced in many areas and change is more likely.

Nurses have the opportunity to share the most intimate moments with patients, whether it involves bringing a new life into the world or sitting quietly with a patient who is leaving it. Patients get well, and nothing is more rewarding than to effect that healing by implementing care that reduces pain, prevents infection, and restores health.

At a time of massive healthcare change with a focus on the bottom line, nurse work continues and, in most instances, is productive and unnoticed. This lack of visibility has been an inherent part of nursing through the years because nurses have wanted it that way. Nurses have never been professionals who boast about their achievements, nor have nurses been interested in the limelight. Their work has been their gratification. Their reward has been in the lives they have affected. Their legacy is their memories of caring. In the words of nurse leader Melanie Dreher (1996), nurses "define their life's work not in terms of a paycheck, working conditions, and employment benefits but in terms of the number of lives saved, families in crisis who were counseled, and patients comforted" (p. 4).

Hospice care is rewarding work even though the nurse might experience six or more deaths in 24 hours. The rewards are not in seeing the patient get well, but in providing comfort and dignity for the patient who is dying. This is known as palliative care. It is alleviating and easing without a cure. Anything that works is right for these patients at the end of their lives. A dollar value cannot be placed on the last few minutes of comforting offered by nurses to the dying patient. Comforting, consoling, and simply being there are the ways that nurse work is provided.

HELPING THROUGH THE FEARS
by Tina Bears

Vic was 37 years old and in end-stage lymphoma (a cancer) and was in obvious respiratory distress. I quickly called his primary physician and was told to place him in a 50% mist mask. His doctor arrived shortly afterwards and after a brief meeting with Vic and his wife Alice, the decision was made to initiate a "Do Not Resuscitate" order for Vic. There I stood at Vic's bedside as Alice, crying, told Vic everything had been done and it was time to be comfortable. Teary-eyed, I left the room to prepare Vic's pain medication. When I came back to the room, Vic and Alice asked me to give them some more time until his family and children came to see him. I felt torn because I wanted Vic to be comfortable but I also wanted him to spend some time with his children before he became incoherent. Here I felt the need to set limits with Vic and Alice. I told them that was fine but I would return shortly to start the medication. When I returned, I still met resistance, but I sensed it was more fear than anything. So I sat with Vic and Alice and told them how the pain medication would begin working to relieve his pain.

After this explanation, they were ready to begin the process. As I punched in the numbers on the pump, an array of emotions flooded me. I felt relief for Vic and his family that his agonizing would end soon, but I also felt sadness that this was a 37-year-old man with three young children and a wife who were robbed of an ordinary life. I told Alice to keep talking to Vic and giving him permission to leave this world. As I ended my shift, I hugged Alice and Vic. Suddenly Vic asked me a question I thought was reserved for doctors, "Tina, how long do I have?" I took his hand and with a tear in my eye explained it was up to God and him.

The next day I came to check on Vic and Alice. Alice immediately and hugged me. Vic was still alive but very lethargic. He did wake up when I was there and I held his hand. I asked if he remembered me. Smiling he said, "Tina I will always remember you as the nurse who made me comfortable." I believe that is the nicest compliment I have ever received. As Alice and I exchanged good byes she expressed her thanks and told me I possessed a very special gift.

PROVIDING PRAISE
by Sara Udell Sullivan Henderson

I had a sweet experience with one of my nursing home residents. He was a 74-year old man named Mel who had advanced Alzheimer's and Parkinson's. We all liked Mel because, even though we couldn't carry on a conversation with him, he was pleasant. He would smile at us and tell us, "Thank you" when we would feed him or give him a drink. All he could do was sit in a chair, eat, and sleep. I'm not sure if he even recognized his family members when they visited.

I was standing at my medication cart, preparing to give someone an insulin injection, when I heard "Amazing Grace" being whistled. It was Mel. He never spoke more than a word or two, let alone whistled. His whistle was strong and clear. He whistled a whole verse in perfect pitch and tempo. It gave me goose bumps because his vibrato sounded just like my father's whistle. When he was finished, I told him how beautiful it was. He gave me a wistful smile and then the moment was gone. Little did I know that it would be the last time I would see his smile.

The next week I came on shift only to discover that Mel was literally on his deathbed. He had left instructions with his family that if his condition worsened he wanted no medical intervention. His wife and two daughters were sitting by his bedside when I made rounds. I could tell by the way he was breathing that he would not live long. The family had requested we keep him comfortable. I moistened his mouth before giving him a small sublingual dose of morphine. I learned in nursing school that the sense of hearing is the last sense to go. I like to speak to people, even when they are unconscious, because one never knows what they might hear. I stroked his hair and spoke a few kind words. I thought the family was very courageous and knew they wanted to be left alone. Within the hour, someone came to get me. She said one of the daughters had come out of the room to say her father had just died. I had been dreading going into his room, but I really felt a strengthening, peaceful spirit come over me as I prayed for help. It seemed a sacred honor to be with the family members at the passing of their beloved father. His body was warm, but lifeless. His wife had tears in her eyes, but somehow I found the voice to speak. "I'd like to tell you about a special experience I had with Mel just recently." I told them the circumstances surrounding the "Amazing Grace" incident and how special it was to me to hear him whistle so strong and clear. His wife told me that "Amazing Grace" was his favorite hymn. I think it was comforting for them to hear this story.

It was only 10 days later that my father died in a hospital room. How I wish I could have been with him! Dad had inspired my desire to study nursing by the example he set as a hard-working, old-fashioned general practitioner. I thought back to the Saturdays when I was about 10 years old, accompanying him on rounds. He would leave me at the nurses' station to speak to the Sisters while he went whistling down the hall to see his patients. On the way home, he would explain the different diseases to me, defining every medical term back to its Latin root, as if I were his intellectual peer. I didn't know at the time that Mel's music was a foreshadowing of my father's death; his whistling an appropriate benediction on Dad's life as well.

Nurses often develop close friendships with their patients that are very rewarding. They do this in a variety of settings and with a variety of patients, for the nurse is someone who cares enough to go to the trailer park or high-rise apartment building to check heart sounds and administer wound care to the foot of a diabetic patient. Since the work world of nurses has no boundaries, their work occurs in schools, clinics, Indian reservations or almost anywhere on the globe. The effect of nurse work on the lives of many is astonishing, as they become friends and confidantes.

MISSION NURSING
Marjorie Culbertson

Mujinga was a female patient in an African mission hospital with a diagnosis of colon cancer. She was to have a colostomy that would not cure her but would give her a better quality of life for the months that remained.

As a missionary nurse, I had been given the African name of Mujinga. The patient was my "shakena" or namesake. In Africa, namesakes form bonding relationships and become responsible for one another.

I knew this 65 year old woman would need much patient teaching and moral support as she faced surgery and the adjustment to the colostomy afterward. I arranged to have the gardener, who worked on the mission station, to come and talk with Mujinga about how he had adjusted to having his colostomy. The gardener shared his story and calmed her anxieties.

Eight months passed, and Mujinga was readmitted to the hospital with problems urinating. She was thin and weak. Her body was debilitated, but her faith in God had grown stronger.

Nights were the most difficult for her because she would have high temperatures and become very uncomfortable. I decided to give my free time to her at night and prepare her for this hard time. This I did by the light of kerosene, in the absence of electricity. While caring for her, it seemed natural to be speaking in the African dialect and sing familiar Christian hymns together. When I left in the morning, we would exchange traditional African good-byes. She would say "waya bimpe," meaning "go well," and I would respond "washala bimpe," or "stay well."

The next few days Mujinga was weaker, slept more, and we did not exchange many words. When she was able to converse, I spoke of her good-bye to me, "stay well," and I calmly told her to "go well." She smiled and immediately we were able to share honestly in the face of her impending death. She relaxed and was freer to "let go." A week later, Mujinga died a very peaceful death in the hospital, with her family at her side. Mujinga taught me that good-byes are not forever. Mujinga remains in my heart. Go well, my shakena.

Patients need care all hours of the day and night, so nurses work variable hours, which are often when others sleep or have fun with their families. This variability is also true for the nurse who works in a clinic, county health department, hospice, or in the corporate world.

Sometimes nurse work does not produce the desired end result. Even though the nurse does everything possible, some patients, as a result of the health condition or the therapy, must face life with disabilities. Circumstances beyond professional control often dictate the outcomes. In such cases, nurses help the patient cope by teaching him/her ways to manage and how to accept the altered self. They exhaust every option to help the patient adjust to life with the disability.

Sometimes they are successful, and sometimes they need to refer the patient to others for assistance. Sometimes, patients die. They are not always old and ready to die. Sometimes they are children, babies and teens, who should have more years of life to live. When nurses witness life taken away by a degenerative disease or cancer, every emotion is drained and every spiritual belief questioned. The physical and emotional pain that patients experience cannot be described. But the ability to ease the pain is a nurse's professional task.

SHOWING RESPECT DURING END-OF-LIFE STAGES
by Anonymous

The first day Mr. Y. entered my path of care was a bright clear afternoon on a cardiac step-down unit in a large hospital in the Southwest. His 10-gallon cowboy hat capped a blue-eyed rugged ranch hand of 30 years. I will not forget the frightened look in his eyes when he said, "I have a heart problem." I knew at that point the days ahead would challenge him as a patient in a whirlwind of health status change and myself as a professional, caring nurse who intended not to lose him in that change.

During the year that followed, Mr. Y. received an internal cardiac defibrillator and every medical procedure and medication for his diagnosis of recurrent rapid heart beat known as ventricular tachycardia. All things changed in his world such as living in the hospital for a year, his environment, his life style, diet, activity, and his social support.

I wanted to create as much of a home environment as possible. Mrs. Y. lived in his room, and we accommodated her in every possible way. The couple needed privacy and intimacy, and I provided the environment for that to occur. The Y's became a part of our nursing village. The staff and I incorporated the "village concept" into his care.

Active listening was a daily practice along with all the counseling strategies of a helping relationship. Near the end of over 10 months in an acute-care setting, I battled daily against his potential for clinical depression. Christmas was approaching, and I thought Mr. Y. would long for his own Christmas party, with all the trimmings. His diet was quite limited, so the cake would have to be made to please him and his cardiologist. I made an egg-beater, low-sodium, low-fat cake and decorated it like a white package with a big red ribbon. The cake, as an intervention, communicated our caring, our understanding of this man in his culture and current life-situation. Mr. Y's eyes absolutely lit up.

Mr. Y. died shortly afterward, but I know his last days were spent in a joyful, hopeful spirit as a human being of worth and with no fear in his eyes.

Nurses often make life and death decisions in the ER, ICU, and neonatal settings. Some say that nurses harden to this emotional roller coaster. That's not true. Rather, nurses build a wall of silence to deal with the frustrations they experience each day, such as incompetence, system defects, and endless phone calls to people who are too busy to care.

For too many years, nurse work has been silently taken for granted. Too often nurses have not taken time to look back on the lives they have touched, and rarely seek credit for their work. Incredible emotional shifts encountered in one work day are considered "part of the job." It is amazing to think that a nurse can spend the entire morning caring for a critically ill patient. If that patient dies, the bed is occupied 30 minutes later by another patient needing the same intensity of care and comfort. As a result, grieving for the patient who just died has to be delayed. While the nurse's heart may be aching for the family who lost the loved one, the job requires making a dramatic emotional shift to heal and care again. And the fate of the new patient, now on the edge of life or death, falls into the nurse's hands.

HELPING THE PATIENT GO HOME AGAIN
by Cathy Champi

It was the best and worst of times for Robert who had probably planted the best crop he had in the 25 years of farming. Suddenly, on a beautiful sunny day in June, he realized his world was being turned upside down. After a very long 2 months of his wife begging him to get a physical for weight loss, Robert thought he would humor his wife and get it over with.

On examination and after a series of tests, a very large mass was found in his bowel and further studies indicated that he was in for the tractor ride of his life. I met Robert as he arrived one afternoon to have extensive bowel surgery for cancer. I can't even remember what type it was, but I did know that it had progressed to a very late stage. The surgical procedure put Robert in a continuous negative fluid balance since there was nothing to absorb the nutrients that were continuously placed in his frail body. Everyone knew Robert had only a few weeks to live and had given up on a lengthy survival.

Inexhaustible amounts of IV fluid were needed to prevent severe dehydration. He was able to take in solids, but what he ate was expelled within minutes into the bag strapped onto his abdomen. The surgeon turned to me for help. With every bit of knowledge I had, I devised a written instruction booklet on the care of his catheter and step-by-step instructions on changing his intravenous fluids. We also designed a device that would hold the weight of the fluid he collected to prevent as many changes as possible. The procedure manual looked crude with hand-made illustrations, but I knew everything he would need to know and do was in those carefully bound pages.

The information was way beyond Robert's knowledge of soil and seeds, but his desire to return home was going to be the catalyst to his learning everything he could to safely care for himself. His independence was very important to him and the only thing he had left to control. So with endless instruction and determination to return to the land and the life he loved, Robert was able to grasp knowledge of his care and return home safely. Exactly 37 days later, Robert was able to walk out of the hospital with his family at one side and his intravenous pole on the other, instilling the precious fluid needed for his "internal" crops. We hugged for a very long time and of course we tried to fight back tears, but like a sudden rainstorm, they came down. 'Til this very day, I can see that old truck as it pulled out of the parking lot and the unforgettable smile on this face. He was going home for the harvest.

Two weeks later I decided to return home to the city. As I left the small farming town, I was drawn to see Robert one more time. I had heard he was doing well, so I decided to take a little detour down Orchard Road on my way out of town. As I traveled down a winding mountain, I could see in the distance a tall, thin, and frail figure carefully rolling an IV pole beside him and admiring his corn stalks as they stood as tall as he did. Nothing so wonderful, at that time, could have hit my eyes and heart. Robert had made it home. Home to the harvest and home to his favorite possession. I could not get myself to go any further because what I already saw could never have gotten any better. I truly saw a miracle.

The work nurses do is constantly changing. It consumes every source of energy and skill that can be mobilized. Nurse work is motivational and fascinating with intellectual demands like those of no other profession. What is learned each day is immensely valuable and becomes part of the experience from which they draw upon for the future. No two patients are alike, and the work is most satisfying. Sometimes being a nurse is like being a detective who's trying to find the clues that lead to a particular action and, ultimately, to the patient's recovery.

GIVING FINAL GIFTS
by Anonymous

I remember when I was a nurse on the progressive care unit at our hospital, there was an elderly woman whom no one wanted to take care of because she was always negative and nothing pleased her. I decided I would take care of her for the day. She had gangrene of the lower leg and she also had a history of frequent episodes of congestive heart failure. She had nothing but complaints when I got into the room and despite my best efforts the first hour, she was still angry at everything and everyone.

Her doctor came in, and after assessing her, explained to me that she needed surgery for the gangrene or she would die from the infection. However, the surgery was so risky there was a good chance she would not survive it because of her heart problems. Before I went in for my next visit with her, I noticed the next day was her birthday. I decided that I would arrange for the cafeteria to make her a cake for that evening. When I went into the room, she told me she'd decided to go ahead with the surgery and take her chances. As I sat there, I could see she knew that her chances were very small. I told her that I was going to surprise her with something tonight because of her birthday the next day.

I have never seen a face light up like hers. She looked at me and said, "The only thing I really want to do is see Fritz. Do you think that's possible?" After an explanation, I found out that Fritz was a German Shepherd she had since he was a puppy. I couldn't bear to tell her that I was planning a cake, instead. I told her I would get her dog to her, one way or another.

I called the neighbors who were caring for her dog to see when and if they could bring him to the hospital. I then called her doctor to determine if there was a way I could remove her heart monitor long enough to get her downstairs to see Fritz. He said he preferred she stay on the unit, but maybe I could take her to the back hallway elevator and let him come up. After talking with the infection control nurse, I made arrangements for Fritz to arrive at 5:30 p.m.

Fritz came right on time. He was a beautiful dog and we were all in tears at the reunion. Barbara was so happy, and you could see Fritz was too! It was a day I made a difference in that ended up being the last day of Barbara's life. I still know it was the best decision I ever made.

Nurse work is diverse and demands an incredible knowledge base and the ability to respond to many kinds of illnesses, conditions, and life-threatening events. Nurses must know the bio-psycho-social aspects of each patient in their care. They analyze subtle clues that cannot always be quantified. Piecing together information—such as "Mr. Smith's color is off today" or "His conversation is different"—are the clues nurses use to save lives. Coupled with intellect and experience, nurses implement skills and assessments that make the difference in a patient's outcome. They relate this information to their colleagues so that each member of the healthcare team is informed.

Sometimes simple reassurance and encouragement are all that it takes to help a patient. Even these diverse skills are not easily learned for they must be sincere, correct, and applicable to the situation.

USING THERAPEUTIC TOUCH
by Katie Johnson

A nurse's bedside manner impacts patients' recovery and healing experiences. Choosing to make nursing an art is increasingly more challenging and easy to overlook as demands on nurses increase. With growing patient loads, it is easy to fall into the trap of simply passing medications and following doctors' orders. Practicing artful nursing includes everything from being non-judgmental to using therapeutic touch to really listening and advocating for the patient. The underlying concept is that patients can tell whether you have positive or negative energy toward them. This impacts their ability to heal. Although many conditions may be alleviated through therapeutic touch, one common ailment that benefits from therapeutic touch is pain.

A few years ago, I cared for a woman who complained that lower back pain kept her from being comfortable enough to rest. I tried everything I had ever been taught. I repositioned her on her side instead of her back and put pillows in between her legs and behind her back for support. I later let her watch a movie, hoping it would distract her from focusing on her back pain. She talked, and I listened as she expressed her frustrations and fears about recovering and being discharged soon. She was in the hospital recovering from pneumonia but had suffered from lower-back pain for years.

Other nurses I talked with said things like, "She's just like that, don't worry too much about it," or "Can you give her any more pain medication?" She had already been given her maximum pain medication and still did not have enough relief. I felt frustrated. Despite any repositioning and comfort measures I provided, she was not comfortable, and the nurses on the unit were out of ideas too.

Finally, it dawned on me to give her a massage, a form of therapeutic touch. At first, she became more tense, but within 10 minutes her breathing slowed and she relaxed her body significantly. After 20 minutes, I knew she was asleep.

She rested peacefully for about 2 hours. When she woke up, she was very pleasant. Before, her eyebrows had been knit together; she just kept sighing and would not hold very still. Now, she appeared calm and was very appreciative. She said she felt much better. I knew our nurse-patient relationship had deepened. I was young at the time and relatively inexperienced. I often felt like my inexperience hindered building a strong nurse-patient trust, but by the end of the day I felt she really trusted me. Her pain ratings on a scale of 1-to-10 also decreased from the 8-to-9 down to the 4-to-5 range following her nap; therefore, her medication dosage was decreased. This patient showed classic documented benefits from the therapeutic touch I provided.

CHANGING LIVES
by Diane M. Ratti

Tammie, 23, was asleep in the back seat at the time of the accident. She was hit in the face by shards of flying glass as the windows shattered and had multiple cuts and bruises on her head and face. She also sustained a closed chest injury. She was intubated and her eyes were swollen closed. Fortunately, she was awake and alert. The ER nurse also told me that none of the other passengers were critically injured and were taken to neighboring hospitals. After receiving word that Tammie's CT scan revealed a chest contusion but no other major pathology, I was hopeful she would be extubated without problems within a day or two.

When I first saw Tammie I wanted to cry. Her face was twice the normal size with hundreds of tiny cuts, and her eyes were swollen tightly closed. Because she was intubated she could not speak but would instead squeeze my hand in response to my questions. I remember thinking how frightened she must be. Throughout the remainder of my shift, I talked to her constantly. I reassured her that the swelling of her face and eyes would diminish, and she would soon be able to open her eyes. I told her that the tube would soon be taken out and she would be able to talk within a day or two. I told her what I knew about the condition of her friends. That night I realized the most important part of nursing care is reassurance and encouragement. I did not see Tammie again until several years later.

One day as I was sitting at the nurses' station reviewing rhythm strips with one of the nursing students on the unit, Tammie approached me and said, "Hi, do you remember me?" Quite puzzled, I looked at her face and quickly tried to remember where we had met, then I stole a look at her name pin but still had no luck in jarring my memory. "No, I am sorry, I don't remember." I admitted somewhat embarrassed. "I'm Tammie, I was over there in Room 5 three years ago. I was in a car accident and you took care of me." As she pointed to Room 5, I vividly recalled the event of that night. Both she and I remembered the exact details. "Your eyes were swollen closed," I said to her. "How did you remember me?" I asked. She replied, "I remember your voice. I recognized it as soon as I heard you talking. I will never forget your voice." I was at a loss for words.

Finally I asked why she decided to become a nurse. She stated that the accident changed her life. The experience of being a patient had a profound impact on her, especially the nursing care. Beginning with the emergency room until discharge, she knew then that she wanted to be a nurse just like me, one who really cared about her patients.

The talents of nurses are true gifts as nurses provide high touch in a high tech environment. They are a calming force when there is chaos. They are knowledgeable, sympathetic, responsible, energetic, and ready to help whenever called upon. They teach patients "self care" skills so they can manage themselves and their health problems successfully at home. They are caring individuals who are there for the patient. Caring is a theme that weaves itself through all of the stories in this book. While nurse work is caring work, it also is being invested in the patient and the family, being dedicated, tenacious (never giving up), an active listener and, above all, competent. It is courageous work. The following chapters develop each of these characteristics by providing living evidence that they exist in the stories of nurses.

REFERENCES

Dreher, M. (1996). Heroism. Reflections, 22(1), 4-5.

ADDITIONAL READINGS

Craft, M. (1996). The many graces of Oklahoma nurses. Reflections, 22(1), 10-11.

Leddy, S. K. (1998). Conceptual Bases of Professional Nursing, 4th Ed. Philadelphia: J. B. Lippincott.

Middleton, F. (1996). The goodness of ordinary people. New York: Crown.

Middleton, F. (1999). The goodness of ordinary people. New York: Crown.

Parker, R. S. (1990). Nurses stories: The search for a relational ethic of care. Advances in Nursing Science, 13, 31-40.

Sullivan, E. J. (1999). Why don't nurses tell their stories? Reflections, 25(1), 4.

University of Rochester. (1998). Woodhull study on nursing and the media. Indianapolis, IN: Sigma Theta Tau International, Center Nursing Press.

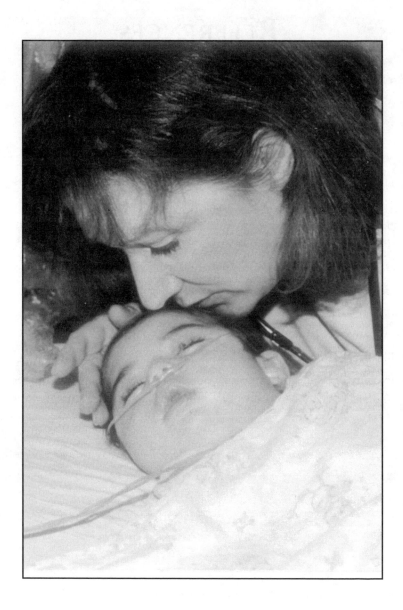

CHAPTER 2

Caring: The Essence of
Nursing

*Caring is central to nursing. It is the unifying focus of the practice
and includes care factors such as;*

- *instilling faith and hope;*
- *cultivating sensitivity;*
- *developing helping-trust relationships;*
- *sharing feelings;*
- *using creative problem solving;*
- *providing supportive, protective, or corrective physical, psycho-
social, and spiritual environments; and*
- *assisting with human needs (Watson, 1988).*

*Caring includes assistive, supportive, and facilitative acts for anoth-
er individual or group with evident or anticipated needs. Caring
includes compassion; concern; empathy; enabling; facilitating; interest;
involvement; health consultation; instruction; love; nurturance; presence;
protective, maintenance, and restorative behaviors; sharing; stimulat-
ing; stress alleviation; support; surveillance; tenderness; touching; and
trust as ways that nurses care (Leininger, 1991).*

*Nurses who use the care factors as outlined by Watson, as well as the
assistive, supportive, and facilitative acts as described by Leininger, help
others by giving of themselves in the most profound ways. Nothing solid-
ifies these concepts better than an examination on how nurses provide
care for children. The following poem, written by a child with cancer and
Jessica McFarland, her nurse, helps one begin to understand how caring
is administered:*

What are children to the Lord? They are angels sent from heaven
and earth. They are like precious stones.

But when one of those children die. You wonder and wonder
why, for children are so innocent they don't deserve to die.

But then we are reminded that children are angels sent from
above and they are down here for a little while to teach us
how to love.

And act like little children and be pleasant in God's eyes. And
when they are gone the memories live in us.

And as for us we try to do the same until the day we die.

The word "challenging" cannot begin to define the work of nurses who care for children, especially those who work in oncology settings. Caring for children means the nurse cares for the parents also. Nurses provide care around the clock to their little patients and their families, meeting the physical and emotional needs of both. When a child needs care, nurses act quickly and decisively. They awaken the primary physician during the night when adverse assessment findings warrant it; they call for lab tests, and x-rays and keep a close watch on the child's vital signs. They cuddle, comfort, and stay with the child. They understand the frightened looks on the faces of the parents for they, too, are often moms and dads themselves. They listen, instruct, and help the parents understand, and, when events warrant more aggressive therapy, they are quick to notice when it's better for the parents to leave.

Improving the quality of life for children in the last days of their lives is difficult work. In many ways, what nurses do in these final hours is very special. They are the energy force and the spirit for the parent. They are the facilitators, clarifying and helping parents get through the worst. Nurses are the ones present at the final hour, often holding the mother as she watches the child she loves slip away from this world.

HELPING PARENTS GRIEVE
by Judy Loeffler

When his mom said, "His little body just can't take it anymore," I thought yes, you're right. My nursing assessment noted subtle changes and decline. I knew his heart wasn't strong enough to last much longer. How could I provide enough support for this young mother? He was only 6 years old. Was he struggling to breathe? Was he feeling pain? Was he able to smile that special grin for me? Was he able to relax from my special touch? These questions and many more were asked over and over again, even in my sleep. During his dying phase, would I be able to hold onto my own emotions and provide the optimal comfort and support to his mom? I scheduled daily nursing visits, sometimes simply holding him, watching him slowly respond to my touch.

I knew his death was close and needed to reassure myself over and over again that I was helping this little guy enter into a new life experience. The day he became unresponsive, I laid his little body next to his mom. As they lay on the couch cuddled together, I tucked the blanket around them. "I'll see you in the morning," I said, as I walked out the door. "Call me if you need me." I arrived in the middle of the night. Mom just couldn't let go. She held him so tightly rocking back and forth, crying loudly. "He's gone, oh, my God, he's gone." The house was packed with family, all so worried mom would never let go, would never lay him down. "She'll let go when she's ready. Just let her hold him. I'll stay as long as you need me." I sat there alone, looking around. Seeing his quiet mobile, his Ernie set on the shelf. As I sat next to mom and child, I could feel our Lord's presence. I knew this little guy could now run and play like other children. He could laugh and sing. He'd never be sick again.

I shared my thoughts and feelings with his mom and knew she'd grieve so terribly. His crib lay empty, never again to feel the fight of life. I hope and pray that some day Mom will remember my words and be able to laugh and sing while her special child smiles down from heaven. Did I make a difference for this family? I hope I did.

Mom chose his favorite blanket, wrapped him snugly, tied his soft warm hat under his chin. I held him so carefully, as I placed him in the hearse. I kissed him so gently on the cheek. "Goodbye little guy, I'm going to miss you."

Caring is more than comforting and giving one's emotions and love. Caring can even mean giving material things. Many nurses use their own money or other resources to help the patient. They buy special shampoo or nail polish for teenagers who do not have a mom. They send flowers to patients who wouldn't ordinarily receive them. They bring food to the patient who is unable to manage until the home care aid arrives. They remember birthdays with cakes and anniversaries with parties.

Nurses care in a variety of small ways. They know the magic of a smile, hug, or nod of approval. They know what a big difference a simple gesture can make, such as holding a hand, rubbing a back, or discussing in simple terms what procedure will occur. They make hats for deformed infants and clothe children in special ways. They draw lips on isolation masks. The feelings, the attachment, the giving are extraordinary.

CARING OUTSIDE YOUR OWN BORDERS
by Anonymous

Fiona lived in Northern Vancouver, Canada. She went to Ecuador with a team of 23 healthcare professionals to help children who had birth defects such as cleft palate and cleft lip. She was part of a group who wanted to give children a better life. She didn't receive a salary for her work, and she paid for her own food, taxi fares, and vaccinations. She obtained supplies so the work could be accomplished.

One of the patients Fiona cared for was a little girl who had a large precancerous mole on her face. The first of a three-stage procedure was done to remove the lesion. Imagine what this did to improve the child's self esteem! Since that trip, Fiona has established a foundation to promote healthcare for children in developing countries.

Caring takes many forms. Several have already been explained. But one of the more subtle forms of caring is just being there.

MOMENTS THAT MAKE A DIFFERENCE
by Jennifer Conklin

Yolanda had been diagnosed with osteogenic sarcoma a year before and had multiple central line placements and had been receiving chemotherapy as scheduled. Yolanda had every possible complication: infections, lines not working properly, etc. She spent weeks at a time at the hospital for each admission. I'm not sure what I expected to see when I walked into her room for the first time, but what I found was a bright 15-year-old girl with blonde peach fuzz on her head, makeup applied better than I could ever do, and wonderful smelling perfume wafting into the hallway.

She had this unbelievably quick wit about her and a laugh you could hear at the nurses' station no matter where she was on the unit. She had a strong spirit even though she had been through so much. Yolanda told you exactly what was on her mind whether you were a brand new nurse or a top surgeon. I spent my first three days taking care of her without a problem. Luckily, Yolanda seemed to like me, so I gave her medicine to control her nausea when she needed it, walked her to the gift shop, and just got to know her. Then on Thursday of my first week, my preceptor explained to me that Yolanda was going to get a certain chemotherapy that day, which she usually had a bad reaction to, such as fever, shaking, chills, and nausea. "Okay," I said. I understood and thought I was ready. I was wrong!

Within 20 minutes of the start of the chemotherapy, we found Yolanda in a fetal position with three blankets wrapped around her, shaking uncontrollably, and with a temp of 102 degrees. She was crying, and it was at that moment I realized that Yolanda truly was merely a 15-year-old girl with cancer. It was also at that moment that my preceptor told me to stay with Yolanda while she went to get the doctors. Stay with Yolanda? I could stay with her, but I had absolutely no idea what to do for her! Then Yolanda mumbled something about her back hurting. So I knelt down on my knees and rubbed her back and told her how great she was doing and that this awful feeling would go away soon. I told her I would stay with her as long as she wanted. When I said that to her she said, "Just a few more minutes, Jen." I continued to rub her back, thankful that she wasn't facing me and seeing the tears stream down my face. When her temperature came down, and the shaking stopped, she fell asleep.

The next day, Yolanda was back to her old self. While I was taking her blood pressure, she thanked me for staying with her the day before, and thanked me a few more times during the day. I kept saying it was no problem, but when I got home, I kept thinking of her frequent thanks. It was such a simple gesture, but the fact that she had it in her mind a whole day later made me realize how much it helped. How much a simple gesture of just being there can make a difference.

CARING BY PROVIDING SUPPORT
by Marty Downey

As a registered nurse and nursing instructor for more than 20 years, many wonderful healing stories come to mind that have strengthened my passion for my work. One particularly touching event occurred several years ago. I was working the evening shift (3-11p.m.) and was assigned to support the emergency department. The evening had been quite busy. Near the end of the shift, I glanced into one of the rooms we were passing and recognized a friend of mine.

Julie, one of the dietitians from the hospital, was sitting on a rollout bed next to two metal cribs. Together, she and I conducted cardiac support courses for patients and families where we taught them about healthy nutrition for successful health when they returned home. Julie taught the information in an interesting and educated manner, making it easy to teach with her. Over the course of the year, Julie happily announced that she was pregnant. We celebrated her pregnancy and later the birth of her twin sons. All seemed quite magical for her. Seeing her in the pediatric department at this late hour, I naturally was curious about her situation. I thought she might welcome some support, so after transferring the pediatric patient to his room and reporting to his nurse, I went back to see Julie.

One look at this new mother, who had spent two days and nights alone worrying about her sons' health, told me she could use some support. Julie told me both boys had upper respiratory difficulties and that a test on one of the twins had been positive for a diagnosis of cystic fibrosis. She was truly distressed and exhausted. She said her husband was uncomfortable in hospitals and felt he could not help. Hearing all of this, I told Julie that I had an hour left on my shift and that I would come back at 11:30 to check on her.

When my shift was over, I went back up to the pediatric unit. Julie had not rested since I spoke to her; one twin or the other was in need of her attention at all times. I asked her if I could hold the fussiest twin so she could get some rest. It did not take much convincing. Julie finished feeding the less needy twin and then showed me how the wires and tubing were connected for the other twin. We lifted him from his crib, and I sat down in a rocking chair next to the crib and monitors, gently rocking this baby while Julie laid down on the cot in the room. The room was not completely quiet, with the beep-beep-beep of the cardiac/respiratory monitor, but the rhythm of those soft sounds soon created a pattern of calm that allowed Julie to rest.

As I cradled this fragile young life in my arms, rocking back and forth, I felt the pain of helplessness that must have been going through my friend. How difficult it must have been to think your perfect child would now grow up needing help to breathe at all times. I wanted to do more for Julie and her sons, but I did not know where to start. Soon, the quiet pattern of rocking and patting gave way to prayer. This comforting ritual filled me with a warm glow. I remembered the many times that prayer was the only thing I could do in situations that seemed hopeless.

Time passed, and Julie rested. When she woke an hour later, she seemed surprised that she had been able to sleep so easily. She said she felt refreshed. We talked for a while, and then I put the baby back into his crib as he was finally resting too. It was close to 1 a.m. I began to feel the strain of the work from the previous shift, so I told Julie I would stop in to see her the next day.

The following day, I arrived early for the evening shift so I could check on Julie and the boys. The nurse at the pediatric unit desk informed me that Julie had gone home for a while. Surely the boys must be doing better because Julie would not leave them unless they had improved. I asked about the twin with cystic fibrosis, wondering if more tests had been done to determine the extent of his condition. The nurse said, "Oh, haven't you heard? The test for cystic fibrosis was a false positive!" My heart and spirit lifted, and I knew the prayers for Julie and her sons were answered. Julie changed jobs, and we soon lost touch. Despite this separation, I feel close to her because of this experience. I have a sense that her sons are now healthy 15-year-olds with promising futures.

Teamwork is an inherent part of nursing. Working together, nurses provide caring of the greatest magnitude. Showing compassion and love, nurses working with families often give patients and families the care they need.

TENDING TO PATIENT NEEDS
by Jessica McFarland

I believe I have had one of the best nursing experiences of my life. After graduating from nursing school I decided to go into oncology nursing partly because I had a good friend in college who had Hodgkin's disease, and partly because I saw second hand some of the effects it had on one of my nursing professors, whose daughter was being treated at the time.

On the unit, with the children as sick as they were, we tended to see a lot of the patients' families and how a bond formed between the families and all the nurses. The unit's staff were very compassionate and cohesive. Everyone knew how the family was doing and structured their lives to meet that family's needs. I have never seen so much strength, love, and compassion displayed as I have with the patients, families, nurses, doctors, social workers, recreation therapists, housekeepers, and other workers on that unit.

A good example of this happened to me while working on this unit, as I became particularly close to one patient. I was her associate nurse, on a unit where we had primary nursing. She was a beautiful 16-year-old who had cancer of her right knee. I remember admitting her. She came rushing through the door in a wheelchair with portable oxygen. She and her mother had just arrived from Florida. Both appeared to be very scared. We got her settled in. The cancer had spread to her lungs and she died 4 months later. But while she was there, several wonderful things happened through the team effort of several people. Not only did the nursing staff help her and her family, but all the other professionals, doctors, social workers, recreation therapists, etc. Through all our efforts, we were able to bring her siblings, all three sisters, from Florida to spend some time with her since she couldn't go home. We were able to get her a personal computer through the Make-A-Wish foundation. We were able to have a beautician come in and apply make up and help her with a glamorous wig, which is very important for a 16-year-old!

As a team of compassionate nurses, we did our best to give this girl and her family everything we had to offer. She, as well as her family, gave us all they had to offer too, namely their faith, trust, and love. I wish I could clearly and entirely describe all the feelings I have about my experiences. I have never felt so much love around a group of people—so much love from patients, families, doctors, social workers, nurses, and all of the other people who somehow touched these children's lives. I count myself lucky to have been a part of these children's lives, and in return having them touch my life and heart the way they did. My life will never be the same.

BEING THE ONLY ONE
by Linda Manley

When thinking of my years in nursing, I think of many special patients, but Michael was the most special because he needed me the most. Michael was an alcoholic, a diabetic, and suffered from seizures. One night he came to the emergency department (ED). He was drunk. While there, he had a seizure with a respiratory arrest. This incident left him with brain damage.

Michael was on our unit several days before I had him as a patient. Michael would become violent at times, not knowing what he was doing. Given his condition, you would not expect him to be sensitive to the feelings of others, but the first day I had Michael as a patient I was feeding him his lunch when I was summoned to the nurses' station for a phone call. My brother-in-law was in the ED with a myocardial infarction (MI). When I went back to Michael's room, he wanted to know what was wrong and what the call was about. I told him I was okay and nothing was wrong, but he sensed my emotional state anyway. He wanted to give me his lemon pie to make me feel better. I was surprised he realized anything was wrong. He remained very sensitive to the feelings of others.

We had Michael for 8 months before he was placed in another facility. He could become combative at times if he was upset or didn't like someone. He did not respond when someone tried to tell him what to do. He hit a couple of staff members. His nursing care had to be provided by 1 person for about 4 months, as he would try to hit others.

I took care of him so much that he learned to trust me. I could usually calm him down and get things under control when he was angry or upset. I think Michael knew I cared for him as a patient and a person. He became so attached to me that on his bad days he would cry when I would leave his room and say he wanted his mommy. The staff would tell him I would be back in a few minutes. He would not relax until I returned.

We had Michael so long that most of us became attached to him. At Christmas time Michael got a lot of new clothes, shoes, toys, and games. I can't single out any outstanding thing I did that was different from what any other nurse did for Michael, but I believe I received more and learned more from Michael than he did from me. I learned that when you give of yourself and learn to care for and love those less fortunate than yourself that you grow as a person and as a nurse. Everyone deserves and needs to be loved and cared for.

Michael was transferred to a facility in Ocala for mentally handicapped people. A friend went to see him, and he was not being cared for the way we took care of him, but they had not yet learned to love him as we did. Michael died about 3 months after leaving our hospital, but he will never be forgotten as long as I live, as he holds a special place in my heart.

The emergency room is a place where many questions are asked and many decisions are made that have ethical considerations. Furthermore, decisions are seldom clear and easy. Many of the decisions are difficult and thought provoking, and many decisions haunt nurses their entire lives. Did I dedicate enough time to that procedure? Was the appropriate action taken? Should a child with terminal illness be resuscitated?

ABIDING WISHES
by Monica Joyce

A phone call was made to the pediatric emergency department that a 10-year-old boy with Downs syndrome, who had progressive heart disease and end-stage congestive heart failure, was on his way in. Neither the cardiology fellow nor the emergency staff had previously cared for this boy. The child was having increasing episodes of shortness of breath, cyanosis, and leg pain. The cardiologist left orders for the staff to assess the incoming patient's oxygen requirements, start an IV, have blood work done, and call him with the results. No other information was conveyed to the staff.

At 4:25 p.m., a boy arrived by car at the emergency department with no pulse. He was not breathing and had generalized cyanosis. A family member shouted, "He is not breathing!" No medic alert bracelet was noted on the child, so cardio pulmonary resuscitation (CPR) was started at the Emergency Room door. The triage nurse anxiously entered the unit to obtain a stretcher and oxygen equipment, and asked for help. A security officer assisted the family by obtaining the child's name and other statistics. He was the boy we were expecting.

He was brought immediately into the code room for resuscitation efforts. The parents were tearful and timidly sat in the front-lobby chairs. They spoke with the nurses about their son.

At 4:31 p.m while chest compressions continued, he was bi-manually ventilated with 100% oxygen with effective aeration. Intravenous fluids were initiated and a breathing tube inserted. The monitor showed rare electrical discharges. Life sustaining medications were given.

At 4:35 p.m. the triage nurse, who had been with the parents, entered the code room and interrupted the attending physician by asking him to terminate the CPR stating "this patient is currently a Do Not Resuscitate. The parents do not want him resuscitated."

I stopped the resuscitation effort in order to support the wishes of the family. The parents told me later they were eternally grateful to me. I have never forgotten them or the meaning that event has had on my current practice. I realized there are many ways to care and to do what is best for the patient.

Terminating care is always difficult, even when it's the wish of the patient or the family. But it takes a particular perspective to realize that the act of termination is caring at its most fundamental level. Sometimes when it seems termination is what is needed, the patient responds and other caring actions are needed instead. The next story shows how one nurse did her best to provide care as a comatose child rallied.

COMFORTABLE QUARTERS
by Jen Kaiser

This story is about a nurse I witnessed on a central-nervous-system (CNS) unit. A 3-year-old little boy had sustained a very serious head injury after a motor-vehicle accident. He was a beautiful little boy from a genuinely caring family. For the first 72 hours we really didn't even know if he would make it. He was on our unit for at least three weeks but did survive his injury. I remember his mother, father, and grandparents keeping a vigil by his bedside. They read to him, surrounding him with all his favorite toys, and played tapes of all his favorite songs while he lay there in a coma. I remember so vividly the day when he started "waking up," and we were able to mobilize him. A nurse brought a rocking chair into his room and asked his mom if she would like to hold him. The mother's eyes lit up and filled with tears. The nurse put the child in her arms. She held him with all the IV tubing, monitors, and wires. She held her little boy.

Nurses often try to change a child's life because they care so much. Caring is, thus, both a service provided and a feeling nurses develop about their patients. For example, nurses have adopted babies with AIDS and children addicted to crack. They have taken children home to celebrate Thanksgiving. They have purchased Christmas and Hanukkah gifts for children. They have even ensured that teenagers received honorary high school degrees. Some have acted as mentors in inner-city communities. Others have dedicated their careers to working in neighborhood nursing centers where healthcare demands are great and nurses care for many underinsured and uninsured patients. These centers originated out of a need for skilled advanced practice nurses to provide health care at a reasonable cost. Most nursing centers are based on primary healthcare models, which means they are community-oriented, accessible, and provide prescriptions and basic lab services. Women and children account for about 70 percent of the visits to a nursing center (Hatcher, Scarinzi, & Kreider, 1998). Many nurses get so close to these patients that they truly love them.

FINDING HOPE WHEN THERE IS NONE
by Sylvia Metzler

He was only 16, but he was my teacher as much as I was his. He was 10 when I met him—loud mouthed, quick to take offense and fight, curious, bright, and painfully honest. He fought the lure of the streets and of our nation's preoccupation with material things for a long time. "I need new sneakers and Payless is having a sale. I don't care if the kids laugh at me. Can I do some work for you?" And laugh at him they did for his name-brand-less clothes, lack of gold chains, and overdue haircuts.

After he'd wash my car or repair some things around the house, we'd buy the sneaks and then maybe take a ride to the suburbs where I used to live. "Where's the trash?" "Where's the graffiti?" "Do they have drive-by shootings here?" he'd ask. "Why are Black people's neighborhoods so dirty and ugly?" So I'd drive him to middle- and upper-class Black neighborhoods and to poor white neighborhoods and talk with him about class and race issues.

When he was about 12, he asked, "Will you be my mentor?" Why would a young Black kid want a 56-year-old White woman recently transplanted from the suburbs to be his mentor? Did he even know what a mentor was? Were my very questions insulting his intelligence and wisdom? So, I accepted this honor with humility and not without a little trepidation.

It was not an easy honor. His aggressive behavior baffled and frustrated his mother and me. His father had been in prison for most of his son's life and was a negative role model at best. His mother struggled to raise him alone and did the best she could. I know he grew tired of scuffling and begging for enough to wear, enough to eat, school supplies, deodorant, laundry money. Things my grandchildren totally took for granted, things all children should be able to take for granted. He was always looking for work, but jobs were hard to come by for adults in his neighborhood, let alone for young Black males.

So he began to sell marijuana. He started to wear nice clothes and buy his mom groceries. He grew tall, lost weight, and the girls started to call him.

I took him to see "Third and Indiana," a play based on a book by Steve Lopez. It could have been about him and countless other young men in the city. The 15-year-old protagonist, Gabriel, gets pulled into the drug world. His mother agonizes and does everything she knows to bring him home, but the streets win and her son dies.

After the play, I asked my student/teacher if it was realistic. "No," he said, "It's worse than that." They pleaded, and begged him to stay away from the drug scene. He did, for awhile, but the lure of easy money and the necessities and luxuries it could buy was too powerful.

His mother called me one morning at 5 a.m. to say be had been arrested the day before for selling marijuana and would I pick them up for his hearing? We spent 4 hours together waiting for the judge. He was very talkative about how the cops had roughed him up, about what he had said and didn't say to them, how he hated jail and would never go back again. During his 15 hours in custody he had experienced beatings, cold, and hunger. The only food he had was a cheese sandwich that he had used for a pillow on the steel bench in the holding cell. We had a good laugh over that.

In the crowded waiting room filled with other young people and their parents waiting for the busy judge, I asked him, "Are you trying to play out 'Third and Indiana'? Either the cops or the dealers are going to kill you." "I'm not going to get killed," he replied, "I'm getting out." I urged his mother and him to consider a stint at a protective center, but the judge released him with a court date set for Monday. That was Saturday afternoon.

Twenty-four hours later, he went back to the drug house, ostensibly to retrieve his expensive sneakers. Four hours later, he was found shot in the right eye with a "dum-dum" bullet. I spent the night with his comatose body in the ICU as his life slowly oozed away—his blood and brains staining the bandages and sheets. I held his hand and told him I loved him, his mother loved him, his grandmother loved him, and his sister loved him and that we didn't want him to die. But I knew his prognosis was hopeless.

He was the perfect candidate for organ donation, but his mother was reluctant at first. Then she remembered his offer of a kidney to his friend. In death, he saved six lives with donations of one heart, one set of lungs, one liver, one pancreas, and two kidneys.

Nurses often care for their patients by being advocates. They speak up for what a child might need. Often there is a monetary problem with an insurance company so the needed care is denied. While challenging insurance companies is a new activity for nurses, they have become very proficient at getting denials reversed. What better practitioners to advocate for the needs of patients than nurses? Nurses understand the needs of patients; they know about their supplies, oxygen set-ups, dressings, and intravenous fluids; they know about the family and their desires. Nurses often successfully negotiate—with much effort at times— the exceptional comprehensive care that is needed.

ADVOCATING FOR CARE
by Sherrilyn Coffman

I spoke with Wanda's mother on the telephone. Wanda was 2 years old and born with a rare congenital anomaly of her lower spine and several other musculoskeletal and urogenital defects. As the pediatric care manager for a large managed care company, my job was to help Wanda get the medical care she needed. As Wanda and her family's advocate, I had often had to explain to my own company why Wanda needed special care. Many times, there were strong emotions involved on the part of the family, as well as company employees and medical providers. I had learned the art of negotiation, communication, persuasion, and above all, listening. I brain stormed with Wanda's mother about issues she would raise at a grievance hearing on overdue bills. I also explained the system of care and clarified the focus of the hearing. This was a tricky task, since I was employed by the very company she was protesting. However, we had developed a level of trust, such that she realized I wanted the best possible care for Wanda, and would be honest as well as energetic in assisting her. I felt I was doing nursing at its best.

TAKING DANGER SERIOUSLY
by Anonymous

I was working at a health department clinic as a nurse practitioner and, while walking down the hall, heard one of the receptionists mention that a young woman was trying to get in to be seen because she had overdosed on Tylenol. This immediately got my attention, so I asked where she was and was told she had been sent to the Department of Social Services to see if she qualified for our clinic. I went down to social services and found her waiting in the reception area. I asked her to tell me her story, and she related that she had broken up with her boyfriend the night before and took 50 Extra-Strength Tylenol tablets. She fell asleep, woke up, and vomited. She no longer felt like killing herself, realized she was out of birth control pills, and came into the clinic to get more.

While she was there, she began to "feel funny" and wanted to be seen by somebody. I explained to her that she was actually very sick and needed to go to the hospital. I told the social worker to call an ambulance. He refused. He said that she had only taken Tylenol and looked fine so it was not an emergency. I told him I'd call one myself. He started yelling at me and I told him to back away from the phone or I'd need to call two ambulances. The ambulance came quickly, and the young woman, who by this time was becoming less alert, was taken to the emergency room and then to intensive care. She was there for several days, but she was young and healthy and survived the experience. I never could get the social worker to understand that an overdose of Tylenol can end in death.

About two months later I was seeing patients when the young woman came into the clinic and said she and her mom had been talking about how close she came to dying and her mom told her she should come thank me for getting her to the hospital in time, so she came by to thank me.

Nurses often have to use advocacy to help a patient obtain a correct diagnosis. Peter was a beautiful, blond child who had begun to lose his communication skills. Peter's mom repeatedly expressed her concerns about his delayed speech and unusual behavior, which included lining up objects and avoiding eye contact. Unfortunately, her concerns were dismissed, and she was considered an overly protective mom. She was told that he was probably just a "late talker."

As the months went by and he still did not talk, the nurse in the pediatrician's office saw reason to be concerned and brought Peter's condition to the attention of the physician. The nurse made sure Peter was referred to a developmental physician specializing in autism and promptly made calls to schedule the appointment. As the nurse and his mother had suspected, Peter was more than a late talker and was diagnosed with autism. He was promptly started on intensive therapy and, in one year, has made impressive strides in both speech and social interaction—thanks to an interested nurse who cared and had great assessment skills.

Providing care often includes using advanced skills. School nurses can be particularly valuable resources to children because they often have advanced skills in physical assessment. The following story is about a remarkable effort made by a mom and an advanced practice school

nurse who went beyond routine assessment to identify a serious famil-
ial problem that affected a child and his siblings. Further, it also is a
good example of how a nurse can help a parent be an advocate for her
own child.

SOLVING MYSTERIES
by Anonymous

I am a school nurse assigned to an elementary school as well as preschool
programs in our district. I am also enrolled in a pediatric nurse practitioner program. Part of my job is to vision screen preschoolers who may qual-
ify for special-education services. I have also taken it upon myself to review
parents' reports of medical issues that might indicate problems.

Nearly two years ago, I did a routine vision screening on a three-year-old
boy. His medical reports were normal, but an experienced preschool
teacher commented that he looked "syndrome-y" and the school psychologist corroborated my observation of bowed legs. Another team member
mentioned that the older brother had worn braces as a child, and the mother revealed that her son's teeth had emerged without enamel. Her pediatric
dentist had told her to mention the problem to the pediatrician but he did
not see it as a problem.

Because I was enrolled in an advanced physical assessment course, I
checked my books to see if there might be a link between teeth and bone
symptoms. Sure enough, I discovered a condition called hypo-phosphatemic rickets. Now the problem was how to suggest treatment without
undermining the family's relationship with their pediatrician. With their
consent I called the pediatrician to get his thoughts about the possibility
of rickets, and he said he did not think the bowed legs were problematic.
But the mom was not ready to give up. I had given her some information
on the condition. So I told her she needed an x-ray of the legs to be taken

as evidence to a specialist. Since her insurance would not cover the specialist without a referral, she asked for an x-ray and referral, coercing the pediatrician with the words "Humor me." Well, to make a long story short, the x-ray revealed hypo-phosphatemic rickets, and the specialist was confounded to find out that a nurse had prompted the referral. The mom and two boys are all being treated for the familial disease, which if it had not been discovered would have rendered them immobile and in great pain.

As I write this episode, I realize that the mom is the real hero because she advocated so well for her son. All I did was put together a few pieces of information and set her on the path to discovery.

SCHOOL NURSING
by Anonymous

Working as a school nurse for a low-income preschool program is an experience different from any type of nursing I've ever done. Much of what I do is preventive care through teaching and screenings. Last year a little girl came into our program with minimal language skills. This child had been seen for regular check-ups but appeared quiet and shy at all check-ups. No indication of any problem appeared on her physical exam, however, we noticed her inattention. I did a hearing screening soon after school started, finding that the child appeared to hear very little. A referral to an audiologist revealed an 80%-90% hearing loss. After being fitted with two hearing aids, this 4-year-old could finally hear the sounds that the rest of us take for granted. Her behavior improved dramatically, and soon her vocabulary increased as well. As a nurse, I made a great difference for this child for life.

Nurses must be able to persevere even when situations are difficult. Some patients reject the nurse and some are openly hostile at times. Most nurses know that they will be accepted and a relationship will develop if they persevere. It is essential to keep communication open when patients are hostile because the hostility is often not about the nurse but about the patient's fears and disappointments.

PERSEVERING FOR THE PATIENT
Teresa M. Conte

A 17-year-old boy with leukemia with central nervous system involvement was being admitted into the hospital. As I walked in I saw a tall, lanky kid that looked like he had been plucked from the streets and put in the room. I said, "Hi, I'm Teresa. I'm going to be your nurse. What's your name?"

"Don't they tell you all of this crap before I get here?" he responded. I was now determined to make it through this! It was confirmed the next day that Allen had relapsed a second time with his leukemia and that this time it had invaded his spinal canal. His physicians had discussed treatment with him and his family the day before.

Over the next weeks, Allen adopted us and we him. We cooked food, bought him clothes, and included him in our families' weddings and other events. His family came when they could, but even when they weren't there, he was never alone.

We saw Allen through a lot over the next couple months, including his anger at having to have a portal for chemotherapy placed in the ventricles of his brain. It looked like a lump in his head and was not stylish. He was frustrated about being sick again after everything he had already been through, and the utter fear, desperation, and hopelessness after his bone marrow transplant had to be cancelled the day he was to be transported to the transplant center because of a fever. The fever kept him with us for the next 2 months.

This last admission was a difficult one for everyone. Allen often cried about not finishing his life and about not going to college. Thinking of what I had learned about grief, I realized he had now come full circle and accepted his fate. His job now was to help us accept it.

One day in October, I came home from work and decided that Allen had given us so much. We needed to give something back to him. What can you give an inner-city kid who has nothing and is at the end of his life? I thought and thought and then I knew the perfect gift—a college diploma.

The next day I called many colleges and universities in the state with what I thought was an unusual but easy task. I did not know this task was going to be so hard. After 5 hours, I realized that I had exhausted every school on my list. I was told by one university official that honorary degrees were only awarded to people of caliber, as if a kid fighting for his life didn't count.

I was determined to get this degree for Allen. I racked my brains. I made 48 calls and got 48 "no responses." There was a yes out there somewhere, and I was not stopping until I heard it.

I called the president of the University of Scranton, my alma mater, and explained the situation. The voice on the other end said, "Yes." I hung up the phone and cried. Allen was going to get his wish.

When I returned to work, Allen was in a lot of pain and on a morphine IV drip around the clock. I went into his room and was greeted as usual. Allen opened his eyes and with a wide grin simply said, "Mother Teresa," to which now I always replied "Son Allen." I took his hand and held it tight. I told him what had happened and let him know that he would be receiving an award for the pursuit of higher education. Tears streamed down his face and he drifted off to sleep.

The next day, on my birthday, I heard on my way to the nurses' locker room that Allen was doing poorly. I went to our charge nurse and asked to be assigned to Allen. At first she looked puzzled. "Are you sure?" "Oh yes," I replied, "never more sure!"

I could not believe how Allen had changed. He was incoherent and lethargic. I went about my usual routine and realized that Allen was not going to be with us for long. I moved his bed into the middle of the room and placed chairs all around. I put his favorite CD on and talked to him. The rest of the day I functioned as the coordinator of care and coordinator of visitors. I encouraged them to sit and hold his hand and I held their hands when they didn't know what to do.

Allen passed away at 7:30 p.m. that night surrounded by his family, the physician and his "other mother" by his side. When I returned home I found a package at my door. It was Allen's diploma. I sent it to the wake with one of the other nurses because I had to work. At the funeral, I saw Allen in his coffin in a stylish suit, with lots of friends around and a diploma resting right near his heart.

The nurses who have told their stories in this chapter do not see their work as extraordinary. It is what they do each day. Yet they all recognize that what they did left a mark on their lives. As they put pen to paper, they felt a catharsis and a freedom to share. They discovered feelings they didn't know they had. The writing alleviated pain and left them with validation of the tremendous contribution they had made to the care of their patients.

REFERENCES

Hatcher, A., Scarinzi, G. D., & Kreider, M. S. (1998). Meeting the Need: A primary healthcare model for a community-based/nurse-managed health center. Nursing and Healthcare, 19(1), 12-19.

Leininger, M. M. (Ed.)(1991). Culture, care, diversity and universality: Theory of nursing. New York: National League for Nursing.

Watson, J. (1988). Nursing: Human science and human care, a theory of nursing. New York: National League for Nursing.

ADDITIONAL READINGS

Bush, H. A. (1997). Critical care nurses' lived experiences of caring. Heart and Lung: The Journal of Acute and Critical Care, 26(5), 387-398.

Donahue P. (1985). Nursing: The finest art. St. Louis: C.V. Mosby.

Green-Hernandez, C. (1997). Application of caring theory in primary care: A challenge for advanced practice. Nursing Administration Quarterly, 21(4), 77-82.

Greenhalgh, J., Vanhanen, L., & Kyngar, H. (1997). Nursing care behaviors. Journal of Advanced Nursing, 27(5), 927-932.

Nightingale. F. (1859). Notes on nursing. New York: D. Appleton & Lange.

Parker, J. M. (1999). Patient or customer? Caring practices in nursing and the global supermarket of care. Journal of the Royal College of Nursing, 6(1), 16-23.

Pusari, N. D. (1998). Eight "Cs" of caring: A holistic framework for nursing terminally ill patients. Contemporary Nurse: A Journal for the Australian Nursing Profession, 7(3), 156-160

Wald, L. (1915). The house on Henry Street. Boston: Little, Brown, & Co.

Ward, S. L. (1998). Caring and healing in the 21st century. American Journal of Maternal/Child Nursing, 23(4), 210-215.

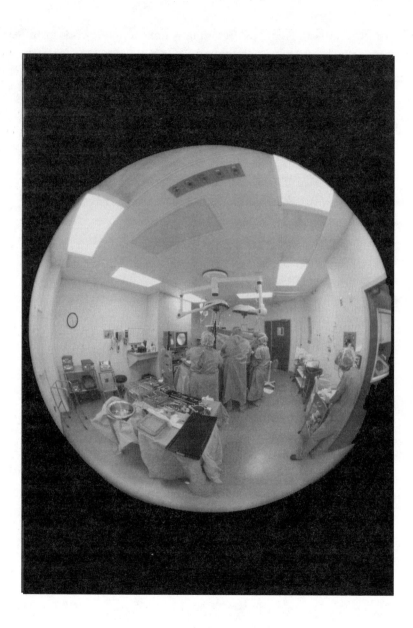

CHAPTER 3

Courage: When Special Action is Needed

One of the most outstanding aspects of nurse work is that, at times, it demands courage. According to the Oxford Dictionary and Thesaurus, *courage is defined as "acting on one's beliefs; disregarding fear; being brave, bold, dauntless, and having 'guts' (p. 322)." There is no better place to witness courage than in the delivery room when a baby is born. Even when the birth is seemingly without risk, problems can arise and lives can be at stake. The delivery room is a place where the nurse is the spokesperson, the decision-maker, and the caretaker of the patient. It is a place where bold decisions must be made by the nurse because the patient is small, unable to adjust to massive changes in the environment, and poorly equipped to cope with the new world without assistance.*

Nurses automatically provide high tech infant care while keeping the mom informed of every action. They also provide support and encouragement to the mom so she can do the work of birthing. This dual responsibility creates tension when the birth is normal. Imagine what it might be like when there are complications. The following scenario illustrates the kind of skill it takes to be in this environment.

CARING FOR THE TINY PATIENT
by Anonymous

Lights are dim and celebration is on hold in birth suite 201. A mother places a loving kiss on her son's tiny forehead before the quiet, limp infant is whisked away into the skillful arms of a neonatal nurse. Carefully, the nurse's work begins as she listens to every breath, timing the rhythms of the 4-inch chest wall. Her attempt to clear the tiny airway by using a bulb syringe doesn't work. She then suctions the baby's mouth "pipette style" pressing her lips to the top of a pediatric catheter. That works better!

As she repositions the pale infant over her hand, he snuggles like a live beanie baby. She administers pulsed oxygen and whispers, "Okay, little one" and strokes a hand that is smaller than a coin. The warmth of heat lamps surrounds the infant in his new environment as his temperature gradually stabilizes. A faint cry, a shiver, a startle reflex, arched back, and suddenly, a whale of a cry. Feet and fists flying, he's fighting to survive. Pink, beautiful pink, skin. His eyes attempt to focus, searching the room in wonderment. The struggle subsides, and the infant bears an angelic, peaceful expression. "You're going to be just fine my friend," the nurse says as she smiles at her new patient and keeps him warm in a knit bunting. She realizes that danger is still imminent and close observation surely warranted, but life has been facilitated.

Caring for infants includes a marriage of gentle care and heightened professional skill. The nurse must be knowledgeable, able to make quick judgments, and do whatever is needed for the infant. She must also help parents with childbirth education, family planning, infant feeding, well-baby care, infant CPR, and parenting skills.

As advocates for women and infants, nurses who care for infants appreciate the importance of the bond between mothers and newborns. They do not succumb to the pressures of routine hospital rules but boldly go beyond the norm to facilitate that bonding. They also advocate for free choice, informed consent, and the dignity of death without machines and artificial support. Without judging, they comfort those women who choose to terminate a pregnancy.

On most occasions, caring for infants and mothers is extremely satisfying work, for birthing is beautiful, joyous, and miraculous. However, the work also is challenging and requires courage. There are times when things go wrong. There are times when the task at hand is difficult and demands that the nurse be innovative. There are times when an uncommon intervention must be tried. It sometimes takes a bold move to get the desired results. In the words of Dr. Vassiliki Lanara (1981): "But above and beyond the intensive stress which characterizes every single nursing moment, what is unknown and incomprehensible to many is the heroism of the nurse's heart which day by day, night by night, creates the unique meanings of nursing (p. 12)."

The stories in this chapter describe the powerful work nurses provide for infants and their families, and exemplify nurses' courage in all of its forms. They are presented as a concrete illustration of the many ways nurses act courageously on a daily basis. For instance, nurses are courageous when they:

- *Do something never tried before that solves a problem*
- *Perform bold and fearless acts for the benefit of the patient(s)*
- *Provide humanistic care when there is no hope for the patient's survival*
- *Act on their beliefs and go out of their way for the patient when it is hard to do so*
- *Intervene when the situation is fraught with anxiety and disappointment*
- *Attempt something that others have failed to accomplish*
- *Continue to offer care when the patient rejects the nurse's actions*

READING THE PATIENT'S NEEDS
by Gayle J. Kasparian

As I reported to work one Sunday morning in November, I quickly looked at the assignment board and saw that I had been assigned to care for the twins. Over the past 3 weeks, since their births in mid October, I had been caring for them on a regular basis. I was becoming very attached to them and their family. Because the twins were born 13 weeks early with immature lungs, they required ventilatory support and multiple interventions. From the very beginning, Twin B required much more support than her sister, who seemed to be so much stronger. Twin A had been weaned from the respirator and had begun a steady weight gain. Her sister on the other hand did not fare as well. Twin B frequently experienced difficulty in maintaining adequate blood oxygen levels. Episodes of slow heart beat (bradycardia) and spells of no heart beat (apnea) occurred frequently followed by periods of continuous drops of oxygen levels in her blood. It was common for Twin B's heart rate to drop dangerously into the 50s. As these events increased in incidence, Twin B had dramatic color changes and profound loss of muscle tone. What little energy stores she may have had were being continuously assaulted and depleted, leaving her exhausted and extremely fragile. Her fragile state required vigilant attention and monitoring from her caregivers.

As this particular morning in November progressed, Twin B had more difficulty maintaining oxygen blood levels above 90%. She was no longer pink but gray. She was also becoming more flaccid. She no longer had the energy to fight back. It was also becoming apparent to me that Twin B was taking much longer to stabilize between these events. In addition, she was requiring more and more intervention.

One of my first attempts to help and support Baby B was to suction her tiny nasal passages. Only minimal amounts of secretions were removed during these attempts. In order to rule out an equipment malfunction, I checked her nasal suction equipment for patency. I looked at the prongs to make sure that they were not occluded from secretions. Her oxygen tube was free from kinks. The flow meter was correctly set.

Whatever improvement I saw in Twin B as a direct result from my interventions was temporary and short-lived. All my attentions and efforts were now being directed toward her. I was no longer able to leave her bedside. I attempted to support her by swaddling her in a bunting. I even tried encasing her tiny body in my hands in hopes that she might find this comforting and offer her some relief from the effects of the devastating morning she was experiencing. I gave her a pacifier, holding it in place with my fingers so that she could suck on it without having it fall out of her mouth. By this time I was becoming more and more frustrated with my lack of success at calming, comforting, and supporting Twin B. I began to rack my brain for ideas. I tried desperately to think of interventions that I had heard about and learned in the Newborn Individualized Developmental Care and Assessment Program (NIDCAP) I had just completed. Twin B was in trouble, and I knew that she could not continue for much longer. Something, but I did not know what, needed to happen and happen soon.

The physicians discussed placing Twin B back on a breathing machine because they were becoming very concerned with her deteriorating condition that morning. Although I knew that Twin B would most likely benefit from this, I did not want her to have to go through it again. Both parents, devastated by Twin B's setback, verbalized their understanding and agreement. Then, very tiredly, her dad asked me if he could hold her. Initially I thought this was not such a great idea. Because of Twin B's deteriorating condition, I silently questioned whether she would be able to tolerate this experience. However, I also knew that her father desperately needed to try to comfort and protect his tiny daughter. As he unbuttoned his shirt, I reached into Twin B's incubator, gently took her out, and placed her against her father's bare chest, hoping all the while that this attempt to revitalize her would work. Unfortunately, the activity caused Twin B to become increasingly more upset. She fussed, arched her back, and began to flail her tiny arms. She became dusky as her blood oxygen levels quickly dropped.

Her dad tried in vain to comfort her by gently cradling her head and bottom in his large hands. He spoke softly and lovingly to her, but his tiny daughter continued to struggle uncontrollably. After a few minutes, the disappointed father asked me to put her back in her incubator. It was then that the idea of placing her next to her sister came to me. Having tried everything I could think of with no success, I decided that I had nothing to lose. Perhaps Twin B's sister could give her what no one else could at that moment. I then looked at both parents and asked if I could place Twin B in with her sister. Simultaneously, both parents responded "Yes." I reached down, took Twin B out of her father's hands, opened the door to Twin A's incubator, and gently placed Twin B beside her sister. Twin B immediately snuggled up against her sister. Her response was remarkable as she quickly began to calm and settle. Her blood oxygen levels soared to 90%.

I stood at their bedside in total amazement. When her blood oxygen level went to 96%, both her parents and I were ecstatic. It appeared that Twin B had finally found what she so desperately needed, to be reunited with her sister. I could see the relief and joy her parents experienced as they pressed against the incubator, looking down upon their two tiny babies nestled together. Their mom voiced her approval by saying, "It makes so much sense. They were together inside my womb. Why shouldn't they be together outside my womb?" As I watched over the twins during the next couple of hours, Twin B's response continued to be remarkable. She was pink. Her blood oxygen levels remained about 95%. Her breathing was no longer labored, and she was finally able to fall asleep. Everything I had been struggling to do had been accomplished with one single act. The frustration I had been experiencing was now replaced with a sense of gratification.

Initially those on the unit viewed the double bedding as a cute social event. But as Twin B's irrefutable improvement was observed, a gradual acceptance of the practice began to emerge, particularly among the physicians. What was once viewed with skepticism is now an acceptable practice within the NICU. Plans to study the practice more closely have been made and since that initial event, five sets of twins, one set of triplets, and two sets of quadruplets have been placed together.

The nurse in the following story did all she could to help save the life of a very sick infant. Her previous experiences provided her with information others did not have and, when she offered a solution to the infant's problem, it was tried with success. It took courage for nurse Kirsten to offer what she did not know would work. It was a bold action that paid off for the infant. Further, her suggestion has become a part of the surgical procedure used with other infants and children with the same problem. Courageous acts often have unknown successful outcomes.

ALLOWING FOR FULL PARENTAL CARE
by Kirsten E. Clary

Debi was a newborn, cherubic little girl. To look at her you would never guess that she had a very severe heart defect. I admitted her to our level three nursery and signed up as her primary nurse. Within a few days we transported her to the local university hospital to undergo the first of a series of corrective surgeries. As I kept track of her status by phone, it was clear she was not doing well after her surgery. One of her lungs filled with air and she developed an overwhelming bacterial infection. The infection severely damaged her kidneys and she came back to our NICU with a catheter in her kidney to support its function.

The catheter was not correctly placed under the skin and gave us problems from the very beginning. Debi was a valiant fighter. As she struggled each day, her nutritional status declined. She developed severe decubiti (bed sores) despite our best efforts, due to her poor circulation. Debi's parents were ever so hopeful. It was my job to support them in their hopefulness but also to assist them in anticipatory grieving. Her nutritional status declined further and the PD catheter began to leak to such an extent that it was impossible to continue peritoneal dialysis.

The surgeons attempted to replace the catheter, but she was unable to heal at the insertion site and so we were unable to keep it in her peritoneum. As the multidisciplinary team met to discuss the pending family conference at which we were to break the news of our inability to help Debi, I just couldn't accept the fact that with all our medical technology and with all the obstacles this child went through, she would end up dying because we could not maintain her dialysis catheter.

I knew the surgeons in cardiac care used a compound called fibrin glue to secure certain catheters in place. The fibrin glue also serves as a "plug" for leaks. Why couldn't we try it here? I mentioned it to the pediatric nephrologist and his response was "Why not?" And, like the characters of the children's book, "Mike Mulligan's Steam Shovel," everyone involved in her care responded "Why not!" She went to surgery and the fibrin glue worked wonders. We were able to resume dialysis the next morning. Debi's nephrologist decided to write up the procedure as it was the first of its kind. We were hopeful that perhaps this little girl would have a chance. Unfortunately, she continued to deteriorate.

Caring for this family required every ounce of my nursing skills. I had to be technically proficient as this child was on a high-frequency breathing machine, had many chest tubes, peritoneal dialysis around the clock and was a challenge in terms of maintaining adequate fluid access. Her skin integrity was about as bad as it could get. I also had to use all the psycho-social skills I possessed. I learned to step back and look at the family as a unit. What would happen to them when they left the hospital? Would they have any positive memories to comfort them in their grief if she died? Would they feel and believe they had been parents to her? In response to these questions, we made Debi's bed space as homelike as possible. Debi's parents performed all of the tasks they would have, had fate given them a different child. They bathed her and rocked her. Yes, even on the ventilator and with all those tubes. They played with her and dressed her in all the outfits they bought in anticipation of her arrival home. Unfortunately, two weeks after the fibrin glue successfully saved her catheter, Debi died of a perforated bowel. I learned the most valuable lesson of my nursing career: the importance of family-centered care. In their loving and caring for her, Debi's parents formed a strong bond with her and so were better able to let her go.

KNOWING THE PATIENT
by Linda Schoene

It was a rare sunny April morning in the Pacific Northwest. The dayshift was gathered while the charge nurse received report and made assignments. It appeared that it would be just another Saturday on the job. Or, at least, that's what I thought. Sarah, the patient in room #1, was being induced at 39 weeks for a fetal demise. She was also a nurse on the postpartum unit and known to all those in labor and delivery except me. I was a relatively new employee and had never met Sarah. Needless to say, caring for patients suffering such a loss is stressful. Helping them through the labor process, trying to preserve memories for them, completing the detailed paperwork, and dealing with one's own feelings of sadness become components of the care plan. For the nurses who knew Sarah, just seeing her name on the board was stressful enough. I looked around the nurses' station and sensed that no one wanted to be assigned to room #1. Thinking that not knowing Sarah might make the situation easier, I said I would be willing to take the assignment.

Totally unprepared for what would happen, I took a deep breath and entered Sarah's room. As I assisted her to the bathroom, my mind was racing.

Could it be? After she was back in bed, I asked her what nursing school she had attended. I then reintroduced myself with my maiden name. To my amazement, we had been in the same BSN program 24 years ago and 2,000 miles away. We had even lived in the same dorm.

As the morning continued and her labor progressed, we renewed our friendship and shared memories of our rather eccentric obstetric instructor. Soon Sarah was ready for her epidural anesthesia and shortly after that she delivered her little girl, Elizabeth. The doctor fussed at me for giving the baby directly to Sarah, but that was what she wanted. I watched Sarah and her husband, Jim, tenderly care for Elizabeth and tried to give them all the time and privacy they needed. After Sarah was discharged, our friendship continued as we bridged the years and caught up with each other. Soon after that I moved to a different state, but we kept in touch. One Christmas,

I received a card that included a picture of their newest addition, a beautiful little boy.

I began that Saturday morning thinking that perhaps not knowing the patient would somehow make the process better or perhaps easier for those involved. As I reflect on the moment I saw Sarah, however, I realize I learned that personal is better. It is the deeper level of the human connection that enhances my level of caring. Working in labor and delivery allows me to be a part of a very personal and intimate experience in a couple's life. Sitting with them during the hours of labor gives me the opportunity to get to know them. As I listen to their story and explore their expectations, I try to make their birth experience very personal. Caring for Sarah showed me that personal knowing is important to my practice.

The next story is about another nurse who initiated a plan that was not accepted by her colleagues at first. But because she persevered and became an advocate for the patient, even in light of the opposition, she clearly performed a courageous act.

CREATIVE CARE
by Anonymous

Several years ago, I took care of an infant with medical problems, who was going to be put up for adoption. His mother did not want to sign off on him until she knew he would be okay. He had no family coming to see him.

Another nurse and I developed a plan that would be used by all of the nurses who would care for him around the clock, giving the infant some consistency. We included a skin care and massage program. Another nurse and I also became very strong advocates for him when dealing with the physicians and their plan of care. I had been keeping track of his growth (his length and head circumference). So I had detailed information for the doctors when I had concerns about their plans for his fluid management.

The patient did very well. He did much better than a patient admitted at the same time with the same gestational age and similar problems, who had a family who saw him often.

When the adopted family brought him back to visit a few years later he looked great! Although some of the other nurses questioned things we had included in his nursing care plan, they followed the care plan. I, along with one of the other nurses who cared for this patient, often felt especially proud of the work we had done with him.

There are times when nurses fulfill a special place in the life of a patient. The next touching story is about a nurse who valued life so much that she made extra efforts to humanize an infant who was not going to survive. When there was no hope for life, her dedication to the infant day after day was clearly a bold and selfless act.

COURAGEOUS CARING
by Debra Woodruff-Capper

I have been a nurse for almost 20 years, but I still remember one of my early experiences like it was yesterday. I was working in a prominent children's hospital in a major metropolitan area and had been so employed about two months. Prior to that time, I had worked 1 year as a charge nurse in a small community hospital on the 11 p.m. to 7 a.m. shift. My unit was an infant transitional unit and I was responsible for seven infants. The children included premature and older infants with congenital problems. One child in particular stands out in my memory.

She was a full-term girl born without a brain and a little brain tissue that protruded through skull bone. She was born in a small community hospital not equipped for an acutely ill child and was therefore transferred to our hospital, about 50 miles away. Her parents were unable to handle her condition and though they did name her, they did not bond or visit. They believed she would not live very long and that it would be best for them to just move on. In reality she lived for more than 4 months.

For some reason, we bonded. I have yet to figure out what attracts people to each other. Over my time as a nurse, I have bonded with some very different patients. Melissa (not her real name) was one of the most interesting. The sac with the brain tissue was on the top of her otherwise empty cranium and leaked fluid sometimes so we kept it dressed with a diaper cover. I did not like the look of a diaper on her head so I bought her a hat that would cover it and dress it up. I cared for her each time I worked and I was never off more than two days in a week. I looked forward to working to be with her and always found extra time to spend with her which was usually during my mealtime. An epidemic of whooping cough broke out in the unit and our room became the isolation room. For better than a week we lived in gown and glove isolation while I drew lips on my face mask so the kids would not think my face was unbalanced. She NEVER contracted whooping cough! Kids in other rooms got it, but she did not. Melissa also did not get infections, but after a time she began to go downhill.

I would come back after my weekend off, and the report would be that she wouldn't last much longer, but by the end of the shift she would rally. It happened time after time, and my co-workers started to comment that I should not care for her anymore because I was doing more harm than good. But I wasn't doing anything extraordinary, just providing love and basic care. One weekend off, I got sick and was out ill on Monday. Melissa died that day. I felt terrible and relieved all at once. I felt like I abandoned her, and she knew it. My intelligent parts knew a life of suffering was not fair for anyone, but without a brain is there suffering? She obviously knew how to feel love and caring, and I'm glad I could provide that for her. To this day I think of her, but when I do it is happy thoughts. Her picture is still in my house. I know I made a difference in this small life.

HELPING A PATIENT GO HOME
by Laura Austin

I work in the neonatal intensive care unit of a large teaching hospital. One of my most vivid memories as a nurse was in my care of a newborn, Francie, and her family.

Francie's family was from a small town several hundred miles away. Her mom came to our hospital to deliver her child. Francie's parents were hopeful for a favorable outcome for their little girl, but the prognosis was grim. Francie was blind, deaf, and had a heart defect that was inoperable.

Francie's parents came to me in their sorrow to say, "We want to take our little girl home." At that point I went to the medical staff to present the family's request. It took several days and many meetings, but it was finally decided Francie would go home.

I taught Francie's parents how to feed her with a tube inserted into her stomach and what to do when Francie stopped breathing. We talked a lot about what her death would be like and how she might look. Finally it was the day to go home. Francie was in congestive heart failure and was on oxygen. But the decision was for no resuscitation.

I helped her parents bathe and dress her. Then we went to the car. As we put Francie in her car seat, her dad said, "Remember, this is a happy day, we're taking our little girl home." I received a phone call the next day from Francie's mom. Francie died 8 hours after getting home.

I still hear from her parents occasionally. Though we don't speak much about Francie, we remember her in our hearts.

CREATING A RELATIONSHIP OF CONCERN
by Malesa Weber

Working as a registered nurse in a medical/surgical "on-call" pool has given me many different experiences. I have dealt with a variety of issues that come with being an on-call nurse assigned to one nursing unit and then another. While this variety is present on a daily basis, there is one thing that remains constant: my love for the interactions with my patients. It is not always easy to find the time to sit down and listen to patients talk about their lives, the frustrations they feel over their condition, or the concerns they have about their healthcare. However, I find every time I do it, I am able to build a stronger nurse-patient relationship and provide better holistic care for the patients.

One of my patients had been admitted to the hospital with an abdominal aortic aneurysm and was going to have it repaired in the morning. He was a big man in his late 60s with a large, supportive family. Different members of his family had been coming and going throughout the day, and my patient had been smiling and pleasant throughout the visits. Because of the many people visiting, I limited my own visits and went into the room only to do an assessment, give medications, and start the essential pre-operative preparations.

After the patient's entire family had left, I went in to have him fill out his history and physical form. The patient looked tired and the smile on his face was waning, but he agreed to fill out the form. The problem was, however, he couldn't see without his contacts, which his wife had just taken home. So, I sat by his side and began to fill out the form with him.

We went through the form, question by question, until I got to one inquiring about his living status after discharge. Tears filled my patient's eyes as he softly said he guessed he would be going home. I stopped and put the form down. I put my hand on my patient's arm and asked him what was troubling him. I spent the next hour talking with my patient about his concerns over the surgery, about death, and about his family. He had received two blessings from family members, which left him the impression that he was going to die. He was already very anxious about the procedure, and he said he loved his family very much, but the visits had made him even more anxious. I spent the majority of the time just listening to him, which made a tremendous difference. By the end of the hour, we both had tears streaming down our faces as he related all of his concerns to me. By listening to my patient, I was able to discover areas where he lacked information. He was very concerned about the surgery and some of the complications involved. Informed consent had already been obtained, but he still had many questions. I explained to him as much as I could, and then I called the doctor and informed him the patient needed to have more explanations about the procedure. While I didn't provide therapies such as guided imagery, hypnosis, or music therapy, I did focus on helping him relax by making him as comfortable as possible. I got him extra pillows, turned down the lights in his room, and tried to make the environment as quiet as possible. These non-pharmacological interventions help reduce anxiety by eliminating external irritating factors.

Generally speaking, support from family members and spiritual leaders help decrease anxiety and grief. My patient was in grief over an anticipated loss of his life. Although he mentioned that the large number of family members and their blessings had caused him increased anxiety, he also stated he was comforted by the fact that he knew his family was supporting him and loved him; when he died, he believed he would go to a wonderful place better than here. His anxiety came because he just wasn't ready to go yet. As we were both of the same religion, discussing our common beliefs seemed to help ease his anxiety.

As he was talking about issues that were very difficult for him, I found touching him on his arm or shoulder really allowed me to reach out to him. It created a bond between us, and I was able to convey my sympathy without saying a word. He was alone in a place in which he did not want to be in, and he believed he was going to die the next morning. Nothing I said could convince him otherwise, but just knowing I truly cared helped him overcome at least a small portion of the difficulties he was going through.

As I sat with him for an hour the night before he went into surgery, I was truly touched. I cared about my patient and his concerns, and by taking the time to listen to him and address some of his concerns, I was able to show I cared. By the time the end of the shift came around, my patient was not just my patient, he was also my friend. The anxiety and grief he was experiencing were massive, and he needed support. I was the one who had to initiate the relationship, though. That night I learned creating strong nurse-patient relationships was the first step in establishing trust, and unity in care, and providing holistic nursing; it is my responsibility to create it.

GIVING SUPPORT AND TIME
by Josephine DeVito

I've been able to see many situations where both nurses and patients were courageous. Recently I was in the NICU when I witnessed a 22-year-old mother and father learning to cope with a crisis situation. Their baby was born with an intestine full of dead cells, and they were waiting for transport to a larger hospital for a small intestine transplant. They were learning about the special needs of their newborn, and the nurse was creating an atmosphere where maternal and paternal attachment could develop.

The parents would stroke the baby, kiss it, and participate in simple tasks like changing dressings over catheter sites, etc. The nurse helped ease this process and gave them time to attach to their newborn. She allowed them time alone with the baby and made herself available for their questions and needs. She non-judgmentally allowed them to grieve the loss of the "ideal healthy baby" that they thought they would have.

FOLLOWING INSTINCTS
by Margaret McGill

I was head nurse of a busy labor and delivery unit. A patient had given birth to a full-term stillborn girl the evening before, and I went to her room on the surgical floor to see how she was and to offer condolences. The patient was turned on her side facing away from the door and had not spoken to anyone since the birth. I sat beside the bed to speak to her and when I asked her if she wanted to see her baby, she opened her eyes, looked directly at me and said, "Can I?" She had not seen or held the child after its birth. She had been heavily sedated and the family decided it was best for her not to see her baby.

This happened about 16 years ago when the research about parent-infant bonding was filtering down to the hospitals and we did not have a "grief team" like so many places now do. Her husband was ambivalent, and her parents and twin sister were adamantly opposed to her seeing the baby even though the baby looked perfect. They were afraid I would make her touch the baby. I was determined that if the mother wanted the chance to see her baby she would, and I told her family that if she reached out for her child I would not deny her the right to hold her baby. I had to go to the morgue and get the dead baby and wrap her in blankets to take to the mother. I unwrapped her face and of course the mother wanted to look more closely and inspect the body and even hold the baby for quite a while. I stayed with the parents and the baby for a long time, as long as they wanted.

We all cried. I have never cried harder or longer with a patient, and I still have tears in my eyes when I recall this experience. I believed then what I know now—that mothers need to see and hold their deceased infants to complete their grieving. It is common now to encourage parents to see their babies, even if they are dead or deformed, but then it was not. And the family was so certain that the greater kindness would be to spare her from the sorrow of seeing and holding her baby. I know that the immediate effect on the mother was that she was animated and communicative for the first time since the birth and death of her infant. She and her husband thanked me. I do not know the long-term effect on the parents of my nursing intervention, but I know the long-term effect on me. I will always consider this terrible, tearful, tragic experience to be among the highlights of my nursing career. I am now a nurse midwife. It's always painful to care for mothers of stillborn babies, but the opportunity to help the family find meaning and solace in the experience and to bond with a child so they can complete their grief work is among the most important contributions I think I can make as a nurse.

FINDING A WAY TO MAKE A DIFFERENCE
by Dana H. Wilson

I worked as a transport nurse. One Saturday, I was called out on a transport to one of the outlying hospitals in the area. The patient was an infant who was born just an hour before, who was very sick. I went by Life Flight to the small hospital and headed straight for the nursery. The infant was in critical condition. After my assessment, I spoke with the neonatologist. He gave me instructions to inform the parents that the infant had less than a 10% chance of survival, but that we would do everything possible to help their son. The family was devastated by the news, but signed the consent for transport.

Once back at my hospital, the physicians examined the infant and did all in their power to help his condition. After several tests, it was discovered that the infant had a genetic renal defect that was incompatible with life. The father and grandparents had arrived. The mother was still at the hospital where she had the cesarean birth. The family stayed at the hospital and spoke with many physicians. The next day, I was again on the transport team when the family returned to the neonatal ICU for an update. The father of the infant spoke with the neonatologist and informed him that they wanted to stop all support and allow their son to die with dignity. I was at the conference when this decision was announced and understood the family's decision. After talking with the family, I found out that the mother was not going to be discharged for another day or two and that the infant would be disconnected and pass away without his mother present. This was very upsetting to me. After speaking with the neonatologist, unit director, and the head of the transport team, I offered the family the option of transporting the infant back to the outlying hospital in order to be with his mother. They desperately wanted that to happen. Our neonatologist spoke with the physician and the administrators at the outlying hospital, and they agreed to take responsibility for the infant.

I quickly called an ambulance and placed the infant into the transport isolette. He had on a white gown which hid all of the tubes and wires that were connected to him. We allowed the father to ride in the ambulance in case the infant passed away while in transit. We made it to the hospital and headed straight to the mother's room. We took the infant out of the isolette and placed him in his mother's arms. She cried as she spoke to him and kissed him. With mom holding her son, dad at her side, and all of the grandparents surrounding the bed, the physician stopped the ventilator and IV fluids. The infant died quickly in his mother's arms among family who loved him very much.

It was a very emotional experience for me and one I will not forget. Since that event, I have received two letters of thanks from the family for my help. They wanted me to know what a difference I had made to the end result of a very difficult decision. The mother and father came by the hospital several weeks after the funeral and expressed their gratitude for everything that had been done for their son and for them. It was nice to see that they were doing well. They had been to see a genetics counselor and had decided to one day try again for a child. They said I made a difference in their life, but little do they know what a difference they made in my life. I will always remember that family and the graciousness they showed me in their time of sorrow and sadness.

SEEING THE BIGGER PICTURE
by Charles Kemp

Jessica came to the clinic with severe onychomycosis—a fungal infection that causes fingernails or toenails to thicken, discolor, disfigure, and split. We had enough Itraconazole (a very expensive drug) to give her one dose, which we did. We then contacted a dermatologist who gave us enough to finish the treatment. The last time we saw Jessica, her fingernails were growing out with no sign of infection. This was a good thing, but Jessica is not really the point of the story. Through the process of treatment, we noticed that Jessica's mother, Maria, seemed distressed. We asked her what was going on and learned that she had no money, her children were going hungry, and her husband had been deported. Lupe, our lay health promoter, helped get the children signed up for a lunch program, and we were able to give the mom some money. Here is the point of the story: Because someone noticed that something was wrong and Lupe was helpful, one of the neighbors called Lupe in the second week of December to tell her that the mom had been killed. The neighbor, Cecelia, took care of the children for 8 days until enough money had been donated to send the mom's body back to Mexico.

The point for all of us is that we need to keep paying attention to what else is going on around us besides physical illness. Because someone noticed, we were able to participate in sending Maria home.

Nurses are often in situations where the patient must make difficult decisions. One of the roles nurses play in these circumstances is to see that the patient has all of the information necessary to make a proper decision. While it might be easy to let patients take the actions they want, the nurse has an obligation to determine exactly why the patient's decision is made, particularly if the decision poses an ethical dilemma. It takes courage to question the patient's wishes and to pose ways for them to reach their desired goal when there does not seem to be a satisfactory solution.

FINDING OPTIONS
by Kristen Haefner

She was a young woman admitted with excessive vomiting in her second pregnancy. I'll call her Beth. Beth already had a young child at home with mild retardation, and she explained to me how she spent every second of every day with him. She was 12 weeks pregnant, and this was her second hospitalization for excessive vomiting. Beth also had numerous admissions with her first pregnancy and had reservations about continuing this one. She was scheduled for an elective removal of the fetus the next morning. As she and I were talking, she became very tearful. Beth explained she did want this baby but could not afford to be hospitalized throughout her pregnancy because her child at home needed her. I could tell that Beth really wanted her child but just needed a little help at home. I got the departments of social service and home care involved, and we discussed options with Beth. With a little help from everybody, Beth was able to go home to be with her son and receive fluids at home when needed and a home health aide to help when necessary.

I never saw Beth again, but it gives me a good feeling to know I made a difference in her life. She would have terminated her pregnancy because she felt it was her only option. I helped her find other options.

NONJUDGMENTAL CARE
by Helene Lynch

I accepted the next admission to our labor and delivery area. The patient was a teenager pregnant for the first time. She was accompanied by her aunt and was obviously frightened, in pain, and in active labor. No one else in her family knew of her pregnancy. Her aunt learned of it only moments before in the emergency department. The patient and I had an almost immediate trusting relationship as I provided her with a nonjudgmental, caring environment. She quickly delivered a healthy baby boy. I stayed with her as she explored the wonders of the new life she produced. She strongly considered placing him for adoption. I gathered resources for her and although she opted to be transferred off the maternity floor for her postpartum recovery, I remained in contact and have since been notified of her high school graduation, marriage, and delivery of two children.

TAKING CHARGE OF THE ENVIRONMENT
by Madeleine Myers

I teach at an LPN program and was on the mother/baby unit. A student called me to the room of a mother and infant. The mother was having difficulty breast-feeding the infant; her infant would not latch on to her nipple. The infant was crying, and the mother looked bewildered and rejected. The night before, the infant had nursed without a problem. The student was anxious, overly enthusiastic to make everything all right. Once I was in the room, I felt tension, harsh light, and loudness. I *felt* the situation.

I took the crying infant and sang softly. I offered the mother warm herbal tea to relax her. When the infant was quiet and returned to the open isolette at the mother's bedside, we repositioned the mother. We changed the light to be reflected off the ceiling so it was less harsh on the mother's and infant's eyes. With a pillow placed under the mother's arm, the swaddled infant was placed to the mother's breast. The eager infant latched on.

Although this reads as though the student and I performed simple tasks, it was the environment that was the problem. Just sensing the overall scheme of things, settling the infant, meeting the mother's needs, and acknowledging the frustration of the mother were paramount.

First the student needed to relax, my being in the room and supporting her was the first of a series of steps which I performed instinctively. The student perceived my focus was on minimizing the distractions and maximizing the tenderness. I didn't take over, rather I was the calming agent.

We were interconnected. We did not tell the mother how to breast-feed. We did not make wise suggestions. We did not offer cliches' or take the infant to the nursery. We literally became part of the healing environment. There were no dramatic shifts, just harmony in the environment. This was one of my most treasured moments as a clinical teacher.

The next story is presented as an example of courage because it demonstrates what nurses can do when others have failed because the patient rejected help. Because the nurse used good interpersonal skills and approached the patient as an individual with worth, she was able to accomplish what others had failed to do. It clearly took courage to attempt to intervene when the patient had made it clear she did not want help.

SHOWING RESPECT
by Elizabeth L. Santley

Combining my duties as a staff nurse in the NICU with my training as an instructor in basic life support skills, I work with a group of my peers in a unit-based program that offers instruction in CPR to parents and care-givers. This is offered as a service to parents of infants who are in the NICU, but this training becomes a necessary component of discharge planning when an infant is considered at risk for developing apnea.

I was asked to provide a one-to-one class with the mother of a pre-term infant in our unit. Opal was not someone you could easily miss. At nearly

6-feet tall with a stocky build and a booming, gravelly voice, she made her presence known. One look at her scarred face, missing teeth, awkward gait, and misshapen fingers told a graphic story of a life that had not been filled with comfort and goodness. Like many other parents who pass through our unit, she came lacking social status and was ever so street-smart, rough, and tough. And yet, she came to us after delivering a tiny infant daughter who was born nearly 15 weeks early and weighed under 2 lbs. She was a 38-year-old new mother, fearful, anxious, and desperately needing what we could provide for her child.

Weeks passed, and Opal's baby grew and developed, not always without complications or setbacks, and some days were easier than others for both of them and the staff as well. Nearing discharge, Opal was put through her paces to prove that with minimal education and financial resources, and even less family support, she could adequately parent her special child. Because the baby still required oxygen and monitoring, Opal was required to successfully complete the parents' CPR class. A special class was arranged for her, her significant other, and another family. The class was difficult at best, and the instructor reported that little attention was paid by any in the group.

All refused to perform life-support skills with a mannequin despite repeated explanation as to the importance of practice. The instructor was frustrated and concerned enough to report what she felt to be an inadequate class participation to meet the requirement for discharge. Days later, after a rather heated exchange, Opal agreed to repeat the class only if she could do it alone. I was asked if I could arrange this, and I agreed. I set up a time with Opal and then I wondered what I had gotten myself into. So many demands had been placed on her. She was angry, defensive, and tired. Looking back, it seemed that maybe we were asking her to jump through hoops to prove herself. Who could blame her for her response? However, if she remained angry, she was certainly not going to be in a frame of mind that would be receptive to learning life-saving skills!

The evening of the class arrived and I brought her into a quiet room and began. She interrupted me almost immediately, but only to thank me for being willing to teach her alone. She felt embarrassed and nervous in front of other people. I assured her that while having to actually perform CPR on a real person would make anyone nervous, the practicing part was just to help us learn, and the reason I was there was not to judge her but to help her know what to do to save the life of her daughter and how to do it! I started over, and Opal interrupted again. She wanted me to know how much she loved and wanted her baby girl! I sat back and listened as she began to tell me that her family had "thrown me away" when she was young. She said she had made many mistakes in her life, had been beaten, robbed, and involved with drugs. Her older daughter had been taken away from her, but she was working harder than she ever had before to clean up her life. She had prayed to God for just one more baby, "please." Now that she had the baby she was afraid she would lose it too.

I reminded her that one way she could work toward keeping her baby was to know how to care for her and know what to do if there was an emergency. She agreed, and we went to work! Slowly and calmly, we went over the signs to watch for, when to call for help, and how to perform the various life-saving skills. She was attentive, receptive, able to explain what to do and why, and willing to go over and over it until she got it right.

After more than an hour, both of us felt she was on the right track, and that she had passed. She asked me to please tell the social worker and her baby's nurse that she had done well. I assured her that I would and that I would "sign off" on the discharge requirement for CPR as well. She stood up to leave, thanked me, and then said, "I like you. You talk nice to me." I took her hand, looked in her eyes, and responded, "You know what? I like it when people talk nice to me, too".

Rarely, have I been so profoundly moved by such a simple statement. Those few words reminded me of how powerful we are in the lives of the patients in our care. How easy it is to judge a person's behavior or appearance. How difficult to put that aside and treat all those we meet with gentleness and compassion. It makes me sad to think that the very simplest of my actions, being patient, willing to listen, showing respect, and kindness, were so foreign in Opal's life. I don't know how the rest of Opal's life or that of her baby turned out. I don't even know if what she told me is true. I do know, however, that she has had a tremendous effect on me. I hope that I always hear her words so clearly in my mind that I never forget to "talk nice" to people. As a nurse and a compassionate human being I cannot think of how any person could deserve less.

The last story presented in this chapter is about a group of nurses who showed courage by devoting their energies to a father who was trying to obtain custody of his newborn after the death of the baby's mother. The special actions this group of nurses pursued, in light of the obstacles facing the father, are a good example of the extent to which nurses will go to provide help and care to a family. Their activities went way beyond what the father expected, and way beyond what is usually provided.

HELPING IN UNUSUAL CIRCUMSTANCES
by Kathleen Gilsbach

My courageous nurses are a group of nurses in the NICU who took it upon themselves to help a father and his baby daughter. Ms. P. was an immigrant from Central America who delivered her baby prematurely here in the United States. Due to her high-risk delivery, she died without being able to name the father of the baby to whom she was not married. As you can imagine, this set up a legal nightmare.

Ms. P's brother lived here in the United States and was able to notify the father of the baby who flew to New York immediately to be with his daughter. Unfortunately, because the mother was unable to complete paternity papers before her death, he had no legal standing as the father of the baby, so the baby was placed in the custody of Child Protective Services.

Luckily, the baby remained in the NICU until the issue of custody was settled, but it took many weeks. During this time the father would come daily to spend time with his baby, who he named after her dead mother. He would hold his daughter for hours on end. Court dates and depositions were taken, including one from Ms. P.'s brother who had to state, that to his knowledge, this man was the only man that his sister was involved with that could be the father of the baby. Through the weeks, this man was adopted by the nurses in the unit. Some brought used clothes from home and other small supplies for the baby. As discharge drew nearer, there was no settlement of the custody question, and a real possibility existed that the baby would be placed with a stranger in foster care. This upset the father terribly. He said, "She's already lost her mother, I don't want her to loose her father."

As luck would have it, by the time of discharge the court ruled the father could take custody of the baby. To celebrate, the nurses planned a surprise baby shower for him. A collection of money was taken to buy baby necessities, such as clothes, blankets, and such. A Saturday afternoon was chosen for the shower. Even the nursing students donated a home-made baby blanket and sleeper. On the day of the party, the charge nurse brought him into the conference room by telling him that there were a few more things they wanted to go over with him in preparation for discharge. Needless to say, he was overwhelmed. First we had to explain the function of a baby shower. "We shower you with presents and then we eat!"

Mr. R. said that all he could think of when he was called into the conference room was "What is left to learn?" He had already practiced bathing, dressing, and how to take a rectal temperature. A few days later the baby went home with her father and paternal grandmother, who had flown in to help take care of her. A few weeks later we got a lovely thank you letter.

Courage in nurse work takes many forms. You have read stories about courageous nurses who have been bold, fearless, persistent and innovative. In some instances, they even had to break rules or boldly try something not done before. Underlying their courage, however, was a deep and sustained belief that what they were doing was right. They were willing to accept the consequences of their acts if what they planned did not work. We can applaud these nurses for the quality of the care provided and for their ability to push forward even when things did not look possible. This is courage.

REFERENCES

Jones, R. A. P. (1996). Processes and models. In R.A.P. Jones & S. E. Beck (Eds.), Decision making in nursing (pp.3-24). Albany, NY: Delmar.

Lanara, V. (1981). Heroism as a nursing value: A philosophical perspective. Athens: Sisterhood Evniki.

ADDITIONAL READINGS

Bishop, B. E. (1996). The world is moving. American Journal of Maternal/Child Nursing, 21, 217.

Coleman, A. (1998). Legacy leadership: Stewardship and courage. Health Progress, 79(6), 28-30, 42

Girardi, L. (1999). It matters to me. RN Magazine, 62, 49-50.

Kerfoot, K. (1999). On leadership: The culture of courage. Nursing Economics, 17(4), 238-239.

Leddy, S., & Pepper, J. M. (1998). Conceptual bases of professional nursing (4th ed). Philadelphia: Lippincott.

Lippman, D. R. (1996). Courage in the line of fire. Reflections, 22(1), 13.

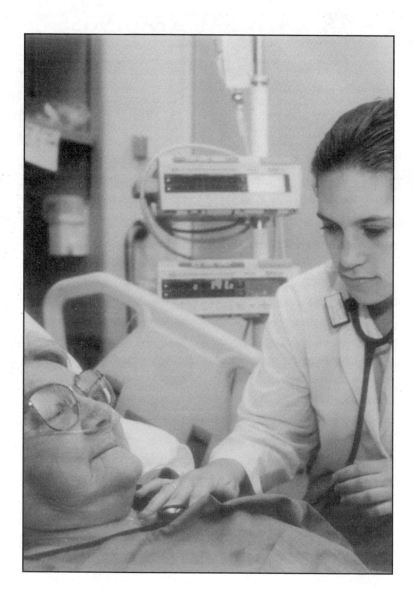

CHAPTER 4

Comfort: The Ultimate Palliative Strategy

Cancer. The very word evokes fear in even the strongest people. People with cancer are afraid for many reasons. The uncertain and lonely path for cancer patients is undoubtedly frightening, as are the treatments that consume much of their lives. Chemotherapy regimens intended to control tumor growth evoke discomfort, alter body image, and wreak havoc on the body. The experience is not easy to cope with. Those who have been healed are afraid of the return of this dreaded disease.

Caring for patients with cancer takes unique skills. The nurse must be able to support the patient during the diagnostic phase, manage the patient's pain and anxieties during the treatment phase, and, in some instances, provide intense physical care and comfort during the dying process. It takes more than caring. It takes more than courage. It takes a special brand of comforting. Comforting the cancer patient means to provide support when no one knows the outcome; to tether hopefulness to the circumstances; to demonstrate empathy; to relieve pain; and to help the family cope with whatever happens. It means giving of self in the most profound ways. It means being strong.

The stories in this chapter are about the work of oncology nurses who have comforted patients with cancer and their families. Their strength, persistence, unwavering devotion, and skilled approach make them a special breed of nurse. Nurse work for them is hard work, but like the work of other nurses, it also is rewarding work. The stories that follow make this abundantly clear.

Comfort can take various forms. There is comfort for the patient in the form of pain relief and there is comfort in the form of being in a comfortable position. There is also comfort in one's decisions, that is, being satisfied that the decision is the right one given the circumstances.

There is also comfort for the family and it, too, can take many forms. There is comfort in what one sees, and there are comfortable feelings resulting from what has been decided or accomplished.

CARING VIA FRIENDSHIP
by Beth LiVolsi

As an oncology nurse at one of the leading hospitals in the country, I saw that it was not uncommon for the nurses to become close with the patients who were often hospitalized for more than a month at a time. I first met Ellen shortly after her diagnosis of leukemia. The 40-year-old mother of a teenage son and daughter, she was open and caring, often inquired about others rather than focusing on her own illness. Throughout her 2-year struggle, I became very close to Ellen and her family. We even exchanged Christmas presents.

Shortly after Christmas, Ellen relapsed for the second time, and her prognosis was quite grim. She and her husband, Frank, were given several options, and they chose to continue her fight with more toxic chemotherapy. After several weeks, she was declining rapidly. She was semiconscious, in renal and liver failure, and had begun to experience some respiratory distress. The doctors approached Frank and explained that she would need to have a tube inserted into her lungs that evening and they were awaiting his consent.

I was Ellen's nurse that evening, and as I entered the room her husband and I just looked at each other with tears in our eyes. "What do I do?" he asked, and I knew he was not asking for the medical advice he had just heard from the doctors. He was asking as a friend. In an attempt to present both sides evenly, I restated the advantages of intubation, and then I told him how it would mean another machine at her bedside, it may or may not prolong her life, and that in the end, it would not cure her leukemia.

By this time we were both crying openly, something I had never done before in a patient's room. We hugged each other, and then Frank told the doctors not to intubate. He then left to be with his children, knowing that the end was near.

Frank called a few hours later. He had gone home and quickly explained the situation to the kids and they insisted on coming back to the hospital to say a final goodbye. Frank was reluctant to have them see her in such poor condition, but he respected their wishes. I told him that Ellen and I would be waiting for their arrival.

I quickly returned to Ellen's room where I bathed her, changed her bed, placed her rosary in her hand, and dimmed the lights. As her family entered her room, I had her and Frank's favorite song, "The Journey" playing on her CD player. Ellen passed away that night. At her wake, a family friend whom I had never met approached me and said "Frank told me everything you did for Ellen that night and I just wanted to say thank you."

It was devastating for all of us to lose such a close friend, a wonderful person who touched our lives. Yet I was proud that at such a difficult time for her and her family, I was able to provide a little dignity for Ellen and a little peace for her family.

HELPING WITH THE TRANSITION
by Mary E. McBean

Every once in a while, I am reminded of why I chose nursing as a career. My reminder came on December 22, 2003, when one of my patients died.

It was a busy morning on a medical-surgical unit, and the staff was working hard to discharge patients so they could be home with their families on Christmas. The feel of Christmas was in the air. One of the nurses had brought in recorded Christmas carols, and they were being played all over the unit.

Our staffing guidelines set "six" as the number of patients that each RN could have, but I had five, and was looking forward to a pleasant workday.

As I sat at the nurses' station reviewing the Kardex, the charge nurse approached me and said that she had to make some changes in the assignment, giving me a dying patient to care for.

I read the patient's history and went to the room to introduce myself to the family and to complete an assessment. As I entered the room, the son asked, "Are you Mary? Will you give my father his pain medication, so he can die in dignity without pain?" I answered, "Yes," and heard a sigh in his voice.

After my assessment, it was very obvious this patient would not last to the end of the shift. The patient's son insisted I medicate his father now and again in 2 hours. After medicating him, I explained to the son that the medication would decrease his breathing rate. He understood fully and made it very clear that he did not want his father to suffer and die in pain.

Death and dying can be a very difficult process for some individuals, but for others, it can be a welcome relief to pain and suffering. And as a nurse, to give compassionate nursing care and support to the patient and family during the dying process is the highest form of nursing. The care I provided that day made me feel good, special, and proud to be a nurse.

Death with dignity is the goal in caring for the dying patient. Giving reassurance in a positive manner that is consistent with the facts is the right thing to do. Care of the dying patient has many facets. The three most crucial are (1) the need for control of pain, (2) the need for preservation of dignity, and (3) the need to preserve self worth, while providing love and affection. One of my primary goals as a nurse is to not only allay the physical suffering of the patients, but also to help prepare them and the family for recognition and acceptance of this reality of life (death) so they can undertake their last task in life with dignity. I know in my heart I did assist in this process, and I made a difference at the point of care. I was a triumphant patient advocate.

Through my own personal experience of feeling hopeless when I was diagnosed with breast cancer, I felt a personal closeness to the patient's family. Dying, and the thought of dying, causes you to take inventory of your life and to put things in proper perspective. Although I never thought that I was going to die because I never claimed my cancer, the emotional fears and physical insults that I did experience were enormous.

The patient's primary physician called and we spoke briefly about keeping the patient as comfortable as possible. Following our conversation, it was time to medicate the patient again. I advised the son to call in other family members so they could be with him at the time of his death and say their final farewells. Within an hour, everyone was present and we all joined hands in a circle around the bed and were led in prayer by the hospital chaplain. As the prayer was being said, I felt a warm rush of electrical current flow through my body, from head to toe. It only lasted for a few seconds, but it was strong and powerful. At that exact moment, the patient died. It was a good death. He died peacefully, pain-free, and with dignity. No matter what is written or said about nursing as a profession, I for one am very proud to be a nurse, and I am convinced, without a doubt, that I made a difference in the lives of the patient's family. My life was affected as well.

Patients experience fear and anxiety, and need to be comforted as a result. They need to feel better even though there may be no cure for what ails them. The next stories are good examples of how simple interventions can provide comfort, and how meaningful even simple acts can be.

EXTRA CARE
by Irene Piazza

As a new graduate, I worked on an oncology and hospice floor not realizing that this would lead me to my current position as an oncology clinical specialist. George had terminal lung cancer and was repeatedly admitted to the unit due to respiratory problems and infections. One evening he was having increasing difficulty with breathing and was close to panic. Despite injections of morphine and Ativan, he was unable to relax. I had earlier encouraged his wife, who had not left his side, to take some time for herself and go home. The unit, as usual, was busy and I had yet to finish giving out my evening medications.

George begged me not to leave him alone fearing that he would die. I dreaded the thought of leaving late another night but knew that I had to stay with him. I sat on the edge of his bed and held his hand for 45 minutes until he finally fell asleep. George died several weeks later at home with his family surrounding him. Years later I still remember that night with tears in my eyes knowing that this is why I became a nurse. George taught me to remember that there is always something that we can do for our patients. We may not be able to cure them, but we, through our love and care, can make a difference in the time left. I also learned from the nurses working with me that night who realized that I needed to be with George and took care of my other patients, allowing me to stay with him. As nurses, we need to not only assess our patients but each other and to offer to help when needed.

SPIRITUAL CARING
by Marquelle Wilkinson

I took care of a man who had back surgery. He had a breathing tube, so he could not talk. He communicated by writing on a "magna-doodle." When I first walked into his room and started doing my assessment, I began by listening to his heart. Immediately, he pointed down to his leg. I looked at it but could not figure out what was wrong, so I handed him the magna-doodle. He wrote that his heart was in his leg—not in his chest, and he smiled at me as I read the message. I started to laugh because he had caught me so off guard. I was very concerned about doing a thorough assessment, but he let me know right off that he was a real person, and had a sense of humor—it was okay to joke with him.

As the day went on, I spent a lot of time caring for this man. He, along with the respiratory therapist and I, walked several laps around the unit. After our last walk, I asked this man if he wanted a bath. He said he did, so I had him sit down in a chair and bathed him there. As I knelt down and washed this man's feet, my mind flashed back to the Scriptures to the account of Jesus washing his disciples' feet. It was at that moment that I caught a glimpse of what it must have been like for the Savior to perform such an act of love. I could not help but feel humbled that, as a nurse, I had an incredible opportunity to wash this man's feet. This feeling was compounded by the fact that he—a man three times my size who was unable to do anything for himself—was humble enough to let me help him.

This overpowering feeling of complete humility stayed with me the remainder of the day, and I couldn't stop thinking about the event that had just taken place. Just a couple of hours before my shift was about to end, this man signaled to me to hand him the magna-doodle. He then wrote a message on it, which said, "You've humbled me today. Thank you and God bless you." I was stunned and immediately told him that he had truly humbled me. I honestly felt I was the one who had been humbled, not him.

Since this experience, I've had several feelings and thoughts about what my role is as a nurse. Looking back, though, I will never forget what I learned about nursing that day. It was in that ICU room that I came to believe that we nurses aren't just performing menial tasks but we are carrying on spiritual work.

CARING LIKE FAMILY
by Nancy J. Hill

My favorite story occurred over the course of my first three years as a nurse. I first met Jeane after she was diagnosed with lymphoma. She was married, had two young children, and was just two years older than I was.

In those days, oncology units did not exist, so Jeane was admitted monthly for her chemotherapy. After we met during her first admission, she would request to be admitted to my floor. She would say that it was her home away from home and we were her second family. Jeane made me realize that nursing went far beyond giving medication, baths, and meeting the patient's medical needs.

I spent hours holding her head when she was vomiting, rubbing her back when it ached, or drying her tears when she just couldn't take it anymore. But for every one of those hours, I spent just as many laughing, listening, watching TV, or being a friend. I met her children and I comforted her sister. Her disease felt as much a part of me as it did her.

There was one particular day when she was admitted to my floor with a severe infection. Jeane did not remember her sister. This was unusual because her sister was always there for Jeane. I walked up to her sister who was very upset and tried to comfort her. Jeane heard my voice and called to me by name. I went to her and she gave me a hug and a kiss and she immediately started to improve. What a strange feeling.

After 3 long years, Jeane lost her battle. I was not there when it happened. I still think she waited for me to leave before she would let go. Whenever times get tough in my career and I question my decision to be a nurse, I think back to Jeane and I move on. I've been in nursing for nearly 20 years and she hasn't failed me yet.

The next story is about nurse Elizabeth and her efforts to help a family cope with, and respond to, their dying loved one. While her actions are not necessarily extraordinary, they are extremely meaningful and an important means for connecting the family members with the dying patient. By comforting them, she helped the family get mobilized so they could reach out to their dying father.

COACHING THE FAMILY IN GOODBYES
by Elizabeth Harrison

Mr. Z. had been admitted to the hospital about a week prior complaining of shortness of breath. He had a lingering cold, and his doctor thought additional tests would be in order. The poor guy ended up being diagnosed with lung cancer. It had spread almost everywhere and his prognosis was very poor.

The night Mr. Z. died, his son Bob came running into the nurses' station and said, "Come quick, something's happening to my dad." When I walked into the room I could tell instantly it would be a matter of minutes before Mr. Z. died. His face was ashen and slightly diaphoretic. His mouth gaped open, and his breathing was deep and irregular. I reached out to stroke Mr. Z.'s forehead and looked around the room for the family. It all happened in a matter of seconds but I've done it so many times it was almost like a conditioned response. I guess I didn't give it too much thought. Bob was sitting in a chair against the wall at the side of the bed. He and his mom were not close enough to the bed to touch Mr. Z. I stood at the bedside noticing how terrified they both appeared. They looked as if they wanted to flee the scene, to push their chairs right out of the room. It was as if terror had a color and it was now painted on their faces.

I continued to stroke Mr. Z.'s forehead and held his hand with my free hand while I asked the family if they knew what was happening. Asking the family of a dying patient if they understand what's happening sounds a little ridiculous, but it's important to know what the family knows, particularly if you are not the nurse who usually cares for the patient. Sometimes you're surprised and the family really doesn't understand that death is imminent. Sometimes, too, we forget that death is a stranger and most people have never watched someone die. How frightened this family looked.

Bob and his mom just sat there. They weren't crying; they were barely breathing. Both looked as if any movement would shatter the scene, and as a result something more horrible would happen. So I told them that if they wanted to they could say goodbye to him. I could tell they heard what I was saying, but fear and grief paralyzed them and made them helpless. All the while I held Mr. Z.'s hand and stroked his forehead. It seemed evident that neither relative was going to budge, so I looked at Bob and told him that his dad would be able to hear him if he wanted to say goodbye or tell his father that he loved him. He could say anything that he thought his father might want to hear. Bob got out of his chair and took his dad's hand. He looked genuinely astounded and said, "You mean my dad can hear me?" I nodded, and he told his dad how much he loved him and would miss him. Bob was crying as he kissed his dad's forehead.

He motioned for his mother to come and say goodbye. She trembled as she reached for her husband's limp hand. Mrs. Z. murmured her surprise on discovering his hand was still warm. Most people expect the dying to feel cold and lifeless, more like a corpse, I suppose. I moved back and she lay her cheek against his and kissed him. She didn't have to say a word. It was all there in her touch.

There is poetry in these scenes, at least that's the way I've always perceived it. They are rare and awesome and beautiful. I've thought that only a poet or painter would be able to do them justice. What I'm talking about is the juxtaposition of life and fading life, of age and youth, vigor and frailty. When I see the hand of the living reach out to touch the hand of the dying, it takes my breath away. It leaves me speechless. It is as if love and comfort were a balm and it was being spread between son and father or husband and wife, whoever is in the scene of sickness and death, loving, and caring. They are saying goodbye, giving permission for leaving, and telling the dying person they will never be forgotten.

Nurses provide comfort through their capacity to feel for the patient and to know what the patient feels. It is through this therapeutic communication that the nurse determines what the patient needs. The nurse develops empathy for what patients are experiencing by actively listening to the fears and questions of the patients and families. Gathering information by listening, touching, smelling, and observing, the nurse is able to determine what the patient and the family need. Good people skills, such as being a good listener, clarifying messages, and delivering clear statements are essential when working with dying patients and their families. Do nurses learn these skills in school? Yes, but being empathic is hard to teach. Empathy must be felt, lived, and experienced, and that takes many nursing episodes to learn.

COMFORT THROUGH EMPATHY
by Candace J. Meares

I was told in report that Charley, age 45, was the sickest of my 10 patients. It was the beginning of an 8-hour night shift. Charley's diagnosis was acute leukemia, and he had been hospitalized several days with swollen joints and an abnormally low hemoglobin and platelet count.

I entered the darkened room. A night light on the wall near the floor by the door was the only light in the room. It was enough, though, and I opted not to turn on the overheads because I could see in the corner of the room that a blond woman was asleep across the seats of two straight-backed chairs which had been pushed together. She appeared to be about my age, was very disheveled and uncomfortable looking. She barely stirred when I entered the room so, assuming she was asleep, I didn't talk directly to her.

I turned to assess Charley. He was receiving the first of several ordered blood transfusions, so I had slipped into his room first for my assessment rounds. I noticed a red leather Bible in the bed. As his eyes met mine and I began to "fiddle" with the blood tubing as I checked the IV site, the amount of blood remaining in the bag, and the rate of flow. I introduced myself and asked, "How are you doing?" I couldn't help but notice how very tired his eyes looked. He told me his joints really hurt and 1 made a mental note to check his medication sheet and orders for the most recent dosage.

From the head to toe assessment, I could see that his joints were indeed swollen. Moving, even turning, caused pretty severe pain, and an area of skin over his coccyx was about to break down. I tilted him toward his left side and propped him with pillows to help him relax into the position. As I progressed through the assessment I asked him if he was a Christian. He nodded that he was. I revealed that I was too, and asked what his favorite scripture verse was as I motioned toward his Bible. He recited it to me. It was one of my favorites from the book of Isaiah.

As I started to leave the room, with a promise to check on the medication situation, his wife said, "He's been passing blood this evening through the rectum." I asked if the doctor knew and she said he did. I thanked her and turned to leave. I spent many minutes next to Charley's bed that night tending to his needs (administering pain medications, antibiotics, and adjusting his IV blood transfusions). On my last trip of the shift into Charley's room, his wife was standing at the sink. She looked pretty awful! I smiled and asked her if she needed anything. Her only request was for a glass of ice, which I gladly brought back for her even though I was really pressed for time. I had such a deep sense of compassion for her, probably because I also had been "the wife at the bedside" 6 years before.

The following night shift, at around 3 a.m., Charley started to bleed from his gastrointestinal tract. We put a tube through his mouth into his stomach and filled it with some iced salt water. The procedure was repeated a couple of times, and then the tube was attached to gravity drainage. I was startled to see the amount of bleeding. As we worked, Charley's breathing changed. The nursing supervisor was paged and came right away. She called the ER and in response a young respiratory therapist (RT) came in and positioned himself at the head of the bed.

With three RNs there, I had the time to look up at Charley's wife. She was sitting upright with both feet on the floor and hands folded in her lap. I could sense her tension and moved over to stand next to her chair. The ER doctor came in and began to get report from the two RNs. I reached down and took her hand in mine. As I stood there it occurred to me that she might not realize the significance of what was about to happen, so I bent down and asked her if she knew what they were about to do. She said, "No" and I said, "They're about to put a tube into Charley's throat to help him breathe."

She looked me straight in the eyes and whispered, "No artificial respiration!" I stood and said aloud, "Mrs. D. says no artificial respiration, Doctor." The doctor looked up and said to her, "Is that your wish or his?" She lowered her eyes and whispered, "Both." The doctor visibly softened and said, "If that's what you want, that's the way it will be." He continued to work with Charley, but dismissed the RT. I encouraged Mrs. D. to go to the bedside. She dropped my hand and moved quickly to the bedside. She leaned over her husband and I heard her say "I love you, Charley and to God be the glory!" And I thought, yes, to God be the glory for allowing me to tread the hallowed ground around the bedside of the dying and to turn my own painful experience into the humbling opportunity to help others during their time of transition.

As I reviewed this memory and assessed this interaction in light of human response patterns, I was able to see that by perceiving this situation through my personal knowing, I was able to utilize my skills in communicating and relating information with Charley and his wife. I was able to empathize and help them choose the manner by which Charley's life was moved from this present world to the next.

RELIEVING PAIN TO FIND THE "REAL" PERSON
by Nikki Hill

Several years ago, I was called to make a visit to a cancer patient who was in a lot of pain according to the family. No pain medication was available that worked very quickly, so a call to the physician gave us quick access to concentrated liquid morphine.

When I entered the home, "Mr. C" was sitting up in a recliner, clutching his arms and frowning—clearly in great pain. I introduced myself and told him I was going to give him a dose of the morphine, and then we would talk. Several minutes after administering the dose, he was relaxed, looked up at me, and said, "You're beautiful." At that I laughed and said, "Gee, I don't hear that much anymore, not even from my husband." He replied with a twinkle in his eye, "Give him morphine."

I did make a difference in this man's life, and his gift to me will always stay with me. Suddenly here was the "real" man—a man with a wonderful sense of humor he could now access. I now use this example often when teaching symptom management and he made a difference for me.

Using an empathetic approach with a dying patient often takes its toll on the nurse. Like the family, the nurse can feel the same pain, loss and grief that the family feels. It takes a strong person to demonstrate empathy and not get so involved that help is impossible. Nurse Pittsman almost took that fatal step but because she knew her limits she was able to be empathetic and useful to Hank and the family as he faced death.

SHARING IN THE LETTING GO
by Tammy Pittsman

One patient, who truly defined why I became a nurse was Hank. Hank had a rare form of lung cancer and had only a short time to live. The first day I cared for him he was awake and alert but became short of breath and quickly fatigued. I tried to cluster my nursing tasks to save as much of his energy as possible because every breath for him was a challenge. His wife stayed at his side and was never without a smile. They were married for over 50 years, and you could still see how much they loved each other. She was eager to share stories about their family with me, and I loved hearing them. We did not really talk about his condition, and the day was very upbeat.

I am part of a "float" pool so I did not see Hank and his wife again until a few weeks later. I received my report from the head nurse for my five patients. The last on my list was Hank. He was unresponsive and now required a ventilator to help him breathe. The physician had discussed his condition with the family and they decided to discontinue the ventilator later in the day and to make Hank a "No Code." I went into his room and completed my assessment as I would for any other patient. Hank's wife stood at his side stroking his face and kissing his cheeks with tears streaking her face. All of Hank's children and their spouses were at his side, too.

I asked them to step out for a few minutes so I could give him a bath. They all looked exhausted and I felt they needed a break. I sent them to get coffee in the waiting room area. I talked to Hank as I bathed him. He looked so different with the breathing tube at his lip, just lying there motionless with the vent breathing for him. He was not assisting the ventilator at all.

I called the family back and I told the eldest son to let me know when they were ready to discontinue the ventilator. I let them have some privacy. I told them to take as long as they needed to say their goodbye. Both the staff and the family felt that when the ventilator was removed, Hank would die because he was not taking any breaths on his own. It was about a half an hour later that they called me to the room. Hank's wife was standing at his side crying, kissing his nose and cheeks, and telling him that she would see him soon in heaven. The eldest son told me that they were going to wait in the "quiet room" until it was "over." Hank's wife walked over to me and I gave her a big hug. I asked her if she was sure she was ready and she told me, "Yes." She asked me to take care of him and I promised her that I would not leave him alone.

I stood at Hank's side holding his hand while the respiratory technician shut off the ventilator and connected the T-piece which delivered 60% oxygen. I stared at Hank's chest as the tears rolled down my face and landed on his sheets. The respiratory tech asked me if I was okay and offered to get someone else to stay with Hank. I told her I was okay and I wasn't leaving, I made a promise to stay no matter how hard it was.

All of a sudden I saw his chest move! It had been at least 3 minutes since the vent was disconnected. I could see Hank's neck vein pounding and then he took another breath. His respirations were six per minute. The tech told me that he probably would not breathe for more than a few minutes on his own. I stood holding his hand for over 15 minutes waiting for the end. I talked to him as if he could hear each word. I told him how I could see what a wonderful man he was by the love his family showed. I told him how beautiful and wonderful his wife was.

Hank's oncologist walked in the room and looked at me. I said in a cracking voice with tears down my face, "He is still breathing." The doctor asked if I was related to Hank. He could not figure out why I was crying. I said "No." I was mad that he could not see the sorrow of losing such a great man.

The doctor left the room and I was alone with Hank again. I stuck my head out the door so I could tell another nurse to look in on my other patients. Hank's sons were right outside the door. "Is he gone?" they asked. "No," I said, "He is breathing on his own." They looked at me with disbelief. "He is a tough old guy," they said and I agreed. I went back in the room alone for another minute and his condition remained unchanged. His respirations were between 6 to 8 per minute and he remained unresponsive. He was receiving medication for comfort by IV and I could increase the rate if he looked like he was in distress. I did not feel it was necessary at that time. He looked so peaceful except for the 6 deep breaths he took each minute.

Without any idea how long Hank would breathe on his own, I went out to the family again. I gathered them all in the quiet room. I explained what happened and I suggested that they go spend more time with him. Hank's wife waited to leave the quiet room until last and pulled me to the side. "I see someone else has been crying," she said referring to me. Of course, I couldn't hold back the tears and started to cry again. This wonderful woman was now comforting me. We stood hugging each other for a few seconds and walked arm in arm back to Hank's room. "I guess he wanted more kisses," I said to her. "He can have all the kisses he wants and then some," she said. I checked in on them every 15 minutes or so and told them to ring if he looked like he was having trouble.

The end of my shift came and Hank was still holding on. His wife was still at his side stroking his face and holding his hand. I wanted to go in once more before I left to say good-bye to Hank and the family. I got hugs from everyone. They all wished me a good night and thanked me. I said goodbye, and I knew I would not see them the next day. Hank's respiration, as infrequent as it was, was now getting labored and the bed shook with every breath. I increased his IV pain medication and told the next shift that I thought he was going to die soon and to take care of the family. His wife had been so ready for the end earlier that morning but I did not know how she would react if he died while she was in the room.

I walked to the elevators and Hank's two sons and their wives followed me. "We know that you did not have to do what you did today, staying with him like that and caring for our mom. We are very glad that you were here today, you made things a lot easier for our mother and we really appreciate it, you are what a nurse should be." I told them to watch their mom, she was ready to lose him earlier and now she would have to be ready to lose him again. I told them I was glad to be there for them and I was really thankful to be a nurse that day. We may not have been able to save Hank from the ravages of cancer but I helped make Hank's passage to death as easy and comfortable as possible for both Hank and his loved ones.

Hank died at 4:15 p.m. that day, less than 30 minutes after I left. I'm glad he held on until I left because it would have broken my heart to see him go. I know his family is doing well and I bet he is watching out for them from heaven.

These stories clearly show the many ways that nurses help patients and families "let go" and start the grieving process. Helping patients die with dignity is one of the most important aspects of the nurse's comforting role. Nurses keep vigil at the bedsides of the dying because they refuse to let patients die alone. In the time that is left for the patient, nurses can make an incredible difference. They touch, kiss and hug their patients when everyone else has given up. They stroke their foreheads in the late evening hours or early morning when the world is quiet. These human comforting skills are very important to the nurse when making contact during a patient's end of life experience. They are skills that often cannot be taught in schools, nor fostered by the sciences. They are part of a human-to-human concern.

Many of these stories have a spiritual aspect. Spiritual comfort is a priority nurses have witnessed over and over again at the time of death. Nurses have willingly met dying patients' requests to read a favorite scripture, say a rosary or recite a prayer. They recognize the need for spiritual peace as well as peace of the body and mind. Wolkomir and Wolkomir (1998) likened the comforting acts of nurses to those in biblical times: "She does not mind that her work, despite the high-tech gear and the life-and-death responsibility, requires services as humble as Jesus' washing of his disciples' feet" (p. 43).

Bathing is a daily activity that many nurses view as an essential part of hygiene and a comfort measure for the patient. To some, such simple interventions as foot baths, hair washing, back massages, denture care and feeding are necessary but not always critical tasks. To nurses who are interested in assuring dignity, these ordinary activities are important ways to demonstrate concern for the patient's humanness while providing needed comfort. Many nurses have stated that the best time to communicate with and teach patients is during a bed bath—a time when patients feel most receptive to learning about their bodies. Providing comfort through the gentle touch of a back rub, a compress change or clean clothes establishes a powerful environment for the nurse-patient relationship. The next story told by nurse Kim is a good example of how clean towels and cool cloths provide physical comfort and are important tools in helping the patient relax and cope with difficult therapy.

BATHING AS A COMFORT TECHNIQUE
by Kim M. Doherty

A 36-year-old active duty military male with newly diagnosed cancer was undergoing high-dose chemotherapy. This man had been very healthy and in control of his life. He and his wife were very overwhelmed with the diagnosis and chemotherapy treatments, so I had spent a lot of time with them to help them become better informed. We discussed huge amounts of information, including medications, procedures, living wills, central-line care, and low blood count precautions. About 1 week into his chemotherapy regimen his white blood count dropped, and he experienced horrible nausea and vomiting.

We tried every anti-vomit medication, but we had no success. Also, he did not wish to be sedated. Finally, I admitted to pharmacological defeat and sat with him and provided just clean towels and cool cloths for this face. I would remain with him while he was vomiting, just rubbing his back. As he was finally able to sleep, I noticed his wife in tears. I immediately tried to reassure her that his nausea and vomiting was temporary. She smiled and just thanked me for staying with them. It meant so much to them both, she explained, to have my support. This happened over a year ago and it still makes me feel so good to think of how important it is to be informed as well as technically proficient. We must never lose site of how critical it is to preserve what makes each of us a nurse.

The nurse activities in the stories presented in this chapter occurred in oncology units, but also take place in other settings. The next chapter presents more about comforting and why it is so critical in helping patients cope, recover, or die with dignity.

REFERENCES

Wolkomir, J. & Wolkomir, R. (1998). The quality of mercy. Smithsonian, 41-51.

ADDITIONAL READINGS

Beddoe, S. S. (1999). Reachable moment. Image: Journal of Nursing Scholarship, 31(3), 248.

Brown, C. E. (1997). Nurses at the bedside. American Journal of Nursing, 97(?), 44-47.

Borysenko, J. (1987). Minding the body, mending the heart. Menlo Park, CA: Addison-Wesley.

Kwekkeboom, K. L. (1999). A model of cognitive behavior interventions in cancer pain management. Image: Journal of Nursing Scholarship, 31(2), 151-156.

Vanderbeck, J. (2000). Till death do us part. American Journal of Nursing, 100(2), 44.

Siegel, B. S. (1989). Peace, love & healing. New York: Harper & Row.

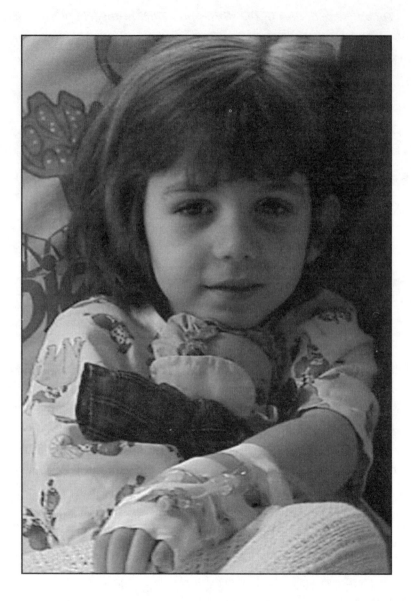

CHAPTER 5

Comfort: Helping Children in Pain Earn Their Badges of Courage

Nurses who care for children are experts at implementing comfort measures. Because of their concern about children and their ability to cope, nurses work hard to make the pain experience tolerable, and the following stories are beautiful examples of how nurses provide comfort for children in pain. Armed with a vast knowledge of developmental norms, along with play that is age-specific, they are able to help children through very painful experiences.

The "comfort basket" is one example of how this knowledge and concern are applied. Utilized by pediatric nurses at Albert Einstein Healthcare Network, a founding member of the Jefferson Health System in Philadelphia, the basket provides comfort that is consistent with the age of the patient and based on the concept that pain management is multifaceted, encompassing aspects of caring, comfort, and diversion. The purpose of the comfort basket is to use toys, trinkets, and gadgets to capture children's attentions and to divert their focus from the pain. The basket contains eye-catching, age-appropriate playthings such as juice canteens, rings, necklaces, finger puppets, and plush animals. For example, when painful procedures are about to be implemented, the nurses reach for the comfort basket. One nurse described the comfort basket toys as "badges of courage." Developmental level, personality, and circumstances were all given careful consideration in the selection of each item in the comfort basket.

The ingenuity of these pediatric nurses is noteworthy. Pain in children was deemed unacceptable and diversion was viewed as critical to success. Strategically armed with the comfort basket, these clever nurses accomplish their goals while keeping in mind the needs of their patients. With basket in hand and warmth in their hearts, they cast a magic spell of intrigue and distraction.

THE GIFTS OF A COMFORT BASKET
by Mary Kampf

I vividly recall the psychological agony of my childhood trips to the dentist. My mother would attempt to calm my anxiety before each visit by discussing what to expect. Then she would remind me of the ring I would receive for being "a good patient." I remember the thought of the gift ring as reassuring. It also strengthened my resolve. Even as a child, I remember trying to live up to my perceived part of the bargain. I wanted to earn that ring. These rings were shown to peers in the schoolyard, and they were respected as a badge of courage. They were worn until they fell apart, long after my finger had turned green.

Now, as an adult, my dentist invites his patients to take a flower from the vase at the end of each visit. I look forward to this modern day acknowledgment that I did what I needed to do and was being recognized. Being acknowledged or recognized for a difficult task is what these gifts are all about. If someone modifies behavior to be an easier patient during treatment because of the acknowledgment they have learned that they will receive in the end, then all the better.

This is an elegantly simple idea that, over the course of time, I had forgotten. So often we go to outside conferences and are reminded of these good ideas but fail to act on them. The pediatric department of Albert Einstein Medical Center can thank one of our staff nurses for bringing home to our unit an idea she heard at a conference. That is the idea of the "Comfort Basket."

After a treatment or procedure is performed on one of our patients, they are invited to choose a gift from our comfort basket. After a long stay, some of our children have quite a pile of these little gifts. These gifts are even more important because many of our families struggle to get bus fare to visit their children, much less have money for the luxury of a gift for that child. These little gifts are our way of acknowledging what our patients are going through. They also help to divert attention from all of the negative things associated with being in a hospital. I have also observed some of our older children being very brave during a procedure as they try to "earn their badge of courage"; even though a gift promised is never withheld because of behavior during a procedure.

After I've offered the verbal sympathy or hugs that follow a painful or difficult procedure, I must confess that it helps me as much as it helps my patient to be able to give them a tangible thing to recognize their struggle. As I analyze each situation, it even helps give closure to these painful situations because of the rhythm that develops with the use of the comfort basket. If the child is able to walk to where we keep the basket, we use this time to further allow the child to gain composure before picking a gift. If they are bed-bound, they often calm down while I go to get the comfort basket. Either way I have found this basket to be a useful tool and all-around great idea that has worked its magic on our young patients.

THE GIFT OF LISTENING
by Mary M. Hale

Irene had been a patient on the pediatric unit off and on since she was three years old; now she was 16. I happened to meet her in the hallway where she had just visited her three-week-old godchild. Imagine, our Irene, a godmother. She had originally come to us 13 years ago via Fire Rescue after a house fire. She was covered with soot and blisters. In the years that followed, she had multiple admissions for asthma.

Our goal with Irene, as well as all our other children, is to reduce the incidence and severity of acute pain, whether it be caused by surgery, medical procedures, or trauma. Throughout her hospitalizations, we could see her altered development due to the stress of hospitalization. She had a loss of independence, separation from a peer group, and altered body image. In response, we assisted her in maintaining her independence by helping her participate in her care. Her contact with peer groups was facilitated so that sometimes we thought the phone was permanently attached to her ear.

Near the end of her hospitalization for asthma, she really began to demonstrate a positive body image through positive statements and behaviors. What could we give Irene from our comfort basket that would foster her new positive adolescent behavior and act as a diversion during some of her painful procedures? We brought the basket into Irene's room and let her choose what she wanted.

She chose a gold-colored necklace and as I sat down to help her put it on she spoke about all the diversions available to her age group: arts, crafts, hobbies, board and card games, video games, T.V. movies, and reading. But, the most important thing of all was how we allowed time for her to discuss concerns, fears, and ask questions; and for us to listen. Her life as a teenager in the hospital had embodied choices, privacy, and comfort. There, in the hallway, when Irene was visiting her godchild, I told her how great she looked standing up and dressed in the latest fashion. Usually on the night shift, she was in bed and wore a hospital gown. She held onto my arm and pulled on the gold colored necklace around her neck and said, "I still have the necklace from the comfort basket."

LEARNING NEW WAYS
by Robyn Carlsen

When I began college, choosing a major was hard because I found it unfathomable to have to decide on the one thing I enjoyed enough to commit to for the rest of my life. When I finally chose nursing and began the prerequisites, it made so much sense. I had been sick much of my life with asthma, allergies, kidney stones, and infections; I believed there was no one better to empathize with those in pain than me. After all, what more could an 18-year-old girl go through? I had been in the hospital more times than all my known acquaintances combined. When I began the nursing program, I was confident in the hospital setting, with the medical terms, and with the seemingly complicated medical technology. I guess I could say I was "prepared" many years before! All of my confident empathy and nonchalance regarding patients vanished one term. It forever changed how I thought about myself and how I interacted with others.

During an oncology nursing course, I arrived at the children's hospital outpatient oncology clinic prepared to learn as much as I could about childhood cancer. We saw the first patient around 8:00 a.m. and prepared him to see the doctor. Matt and his mother were waiting inside one of the exam rooms. The nurse had prepared me to see the patient by telling me about the patient's disease, history, and reason for the visit while walking to the room. Matt was a 7-year-old who had been diagnosed with leukemia over a year ago. The disease had gone into remission, only to appear again a month ago. At the beginning of every patient's new treatment cycle, he or she is given a treatment calendar that displays all the different injections, chemotherapy, and radiation appointments scattered over the next few weeks.

As I went over all of the appointments with Matt and his mother, something sprang alive inside me. Big eyes, scrapes on his knees, and dirty hands all contributed to the picture worthy of a Saturday Evening Post cover. Matt was old enough to know what was happening to his young body. He had not yet had a chance to attend school without this diagnosis hanging over his head. He was learning to read from the books that were stacked next to the IV poles and learning to tell time from the clocks that hung over his chemotherapy. It was an uncertain future for a boy who had barely had time to dream.

I began to think about all the things he needed and how little my nursing knowledge and hospital experience mattered to this boy with a potentially fatal disease. I knew my controlled asthma, antibiotics, and dreams for the future were not the things that were going to enable me to sympathize with and help him. There was nothing I had experienced that would compare to the courage this boy was already required to show the world because of the harsh regular treatments he had to endure and the unsure future he had to look forward to.

As a student, I had extra time to spend with patients, and I quickly learned pediatric patients love to play games. I played checkers with him to pass the time. When waiting for a doctor or for a treatment to end, it always seemed like the minutes stretched on for days. I was never very good at checkers and when he beat me for the second time in a row, I smiled and threw up my hands in defeat. "Why do I try playing against a master? You are just too good. Tell me your secrets!" He giggled and looked at me innocently while setting up the checkers for another triumph. We played until his mother got back from lunch, the treatment was over, and he had to leave. I waved goodbye and was rewarded with a blue smile— the byproduct of a large sucker.

I knew the things I had previously relied on to give me the credentials needed to survive nursing heartache and triumph day after day did not include a special insight into hospitalization. I wanted all the patients who were facing the unknown to know that although I had not experienced the many things they were dealing with, I did have something more than understanding: I had love.

The comfort basket has many uses. It not only provides diversion, it also rewards children for good behavior. It gives children a reason to be strong, to sustain the painful experience, and provides visible evidence of their fortitude. Collecting items from the comfort basket demonstrates how the child has been able to cope successfully with pain and other difficult experiences over time. The items in the comfort basket are also good ways to keep children occupied when they are alone and unable to be comforted by their family.

HELPING REDUCE STRESS
by Ruth Noesner

Whenever we work the July 4th weekend, there are a few fireworks accidents. I received such an admission on Saturday night. He was 13 years old. He had found a firecracker in the backyard, and it exploded in his hand. He lost part of his thumb, all of his index finger, a part of his second finger, and had a deep wound in his palm.

Hand surgeries are painful, and he was on a patient-controlled analgesia pump. He was receiving IV fluids and his injured hand was in a vertical sling, elevated on a pole. To understand him a little better you have to know part of his medical history. He had Attention Deficit Hyperactivity Disorder (ADHD). We have found that the worst thing you can do to these children is to require them to be still and alone. No one came to the floor with him when he was admitted. His family left the hospital while he was in the recovery room. We placed him in a semi-private room, but he had no roommate. When he fully recovered from anesthesia in the middle of the night, his injured arm was in the vertical sling on the one side and the other arm was connected to two different pumps, which both alarmed when he bent his elbow. My challenge for the rest of the night was to hope that morning arrived without disconnection of the IV lines and further injury to his postoperative wounds.

I spent most of the night shift from 2 a.m. to 7 a.m. in that room with him. We checked out the comfort basket for something that would be age-appropriate and diversional for him. He chose a Beeper Bubble Gum Pack and playing cards. He was delighted with his prizes, especially that they were his to keep. We played cards off and on for the rest of the night. When I had to attend to my other patients, I would tell him what I had to do, and he would be calling out frantically in less than 2 minutes, very pleasantly and politely but still demanding. Thanks to the comfort basket, I was able to help reduce the pain and stress associated with his hospitalization.

The items in the comfort basket can also relieve anxiety by camouflaging frightening therapies. The story of John and Henry is an excellent example of how versatile the comfort basket can be for reducing anxiety and psychic pain.

HELPING TO DIVERT ATTENTION AND PAIN
by Joanne Slutsky

"John Henry was a steel-driving man." Those were the words that went through my mind when I first met John and Henry. But in my case, John Henry turned out to be steel-driven boys. Let me explain. In May, we were informed that the pediatric floor would be receiving two motor vehicle accident victims. One, Henry, was a nine-year-old and the other, John, was a 16-year-old. The boys had been riding on a motor bike when it was struck by a car careening around a corner. Both boys suffered right femur fractures. Both boys were in the operating room for approximately two to four hours and both boys would be wearing external fixator devices for quite some time. This required dressing changes twice a day; six pin sites for Henry and eight pin sites for John. The two young boys were well medicated prior to the pin cleaning. While that may have lessened their actual pain, it did not alleviate the emotional discomfort of seeing steel rods going in one side of the leg and coming out the other. The surgeons, well aware of the initial psychological impact such a sight would have, sent both boys back from the operating room with the devices well wrapped in bandages. When we first removed the bandages from John's leg, Henry, in the next bed, was able to see how the "erector set" was built around his friend's leg. Henry's reaction was immediate and unstoppable. He leaned over his bed rails and vomited. John, the older boy, did not go as far as Henry, but he was extremely apprehensive and vocal about his dislike of having any part of his leg or the device touched.

John and Henry's fear and apprehension were understandable and appropriate. But, except for medicating them, which was done, and reassuring them that we would be as gentle as possible, which we were, there was not much else we could do. I spent a great deal of time with both boys and their parents, explaining the procedures and attempting to lessen their fears. Then I remembered our "Comfort Basket." What could that "basket" hold for a pre-teen and a teenager? It had coloring books, crayons, bubbles, "slinkies," rattles, and baby toys. Then I saw them; a collection of rubber-jelly finger puppets!

John and Henry had to have their pin sites cleaned twice a day. They were promised a finger puppet for each cleaning. By the end of five days, they would have enough for all ten fingers. I guaranteed them that by the time they had a full puppet hand, the pin care would be much less oner-ous. Instead of scoffing at the idea, both boys enthusiastically agreed.

Those finger puppets did the trick! Yes, they continued to be medicat-ed and yes, they continued to voice their concerns; but that now was somewhat mitigated by the anticipation of receiving additional little pup-pets for their collection. By the third day, both John and Henry were assist-ing with the pin cleaning. By the fifth day, Henry said, "Remember when you told us that it was going to get better? Well, you were right and when I'm home, I'll be able to do my own pin cleaning."

The boys were very possessive of their finger puppets. Once, somebody had come into their room while they were down at Physical Therapy and had "thoughtfully" cleared the bedside table of extraneous materials. Upon their return to their room, there ensued quite a vocal discussion of who had taken their puppets. Luckily, they were found in the bedside drawers. John and Henry, our steel-driven boys, took those finger puppets home with them. Both the external fixator and those silly little rubber toys became symbols of their triumph.

Items from the comfort basket are not the only way to distract chil-dren who are in pain. There are many toys that can be used to keep chil-dren comfortable when they are not able to romp and run or are in pain and frightened by the situation and therapy. Clark, a five-year old, learned about a different kind of therapy when given a toy from the comfort basket.

Tactics for Helping Patients Help Themselves
by Mary M. Hale

Clark was 5 years old when he was hit by a car while roller-blading. The car had to be lifted off of his left leg. He sustained a fractured left leg and multiple abrasions to his right ear, face, and right shoulder. Clark was very special to his parents because he was their only son. During the first few months of his life, he had been in and out of the hospital a lot.

Clark was with us about 3 weeks. His first and foremost problem was pain. He was in skeletal traction and needed frequent pin care and neuro-vascular checks which were new and scary to Clark. What could we give him from our comfort basket that would be a diversion? Because Clark was reluctant to take fluids, we gave him a drinking cup like a yellow Crayola crayon. He would not touch it at first, then began to weaken. He enjoyed a simple game involving his special cup and eventually began to drink from it.

His skeletal traction suspended him in space and tended to shift his alignment so that he had to be repositioned frequently. When he began to have nightmares, we worked with family members and Clark to ease his fears. He began to be more and more dependent on his family and our staff. Self-help development was on hold until one of the staff nurses brought in "Daddy Long-Legs" to hang from his traction apparatus. It was a cardboard "scarecrow" with 2-foot long tubular legs filled with bubble gum.

Clark let Daddy Long Legs hang on his traction for a few days without comment. Then his play skills took over. He even tried to open the legs to get at the bubble gum. You could see him thinking when he finally was able to chew small amounts of the gum. He asked his mother and one of the care givers, "Can I use bubble gum to paste my leg back together?" "Not yet, Clark," was the reply. "Maybe by the time you grow up and become a bone doctor that will be the treatment of choice." Clark went home to a loving family but is not back to roller-blading yet.

Mr. Lemon, a toy from the comfort basket, played a major role in the management of pain for Eddy, an 11-year old who was hospitalized for a tonsillectomy and adenoidectomy. His story, told by nurse Mary, is more evidence that comfort can be provided by diversion.

CONVINCING A YOUNG PATIENT TO HELP
by Mary M. Hale

Eddy, age 11, was admitted to the pediatric unit postoperatively, after a tonsillectomy and adenoidectomy. He had the "dreaded" I.V. and was not drinking fluids. Eddy was receiving IV medications for his pain, but was very anxious. He was tall for his age, and never far from his mother. Eddy's mom was one week post-op from a hysterectomy and was spending the night with Eddy.

He had great difficulty in getting to sleep in a strange bed. We had recommended that the family bring in familiar objects to remind the patient of home and family. We discussed several appropriate interventions with the mother and involved his parents in his care. Nothing seemed to work. Then I thought of the comfort basket. We had one plush toy, a "Mr. Lemon" with a smiley face.

We are well aware of the goals of pain management for children: reduce the incidence and severity of children's acute pain; educate children and their families to communicate about pain, enhance the child's comfort and increase the child's and the family's satisfaction with pain management, reduce postoperative complications, and reduce the length of hospital stay. We had to combine pharmacologic and non-pharmacologic options as appropriate.

We also had to deal with altered development related to the stress of hospitalization such as separation from peer group, boredom, and decreased opportunity to achieve mastery. Eddy's mother also understood the importance of diversion and we were both pleased when Eddy bonded immediately with "Mister Lemon." Mom stated that she thought it was the toy's smile. For myself, I'm not so sure. It could have been Eddy's love for lemonade. Early in the morning he started to drink—lemonade —of course!

Creatively Convincing Toddlers to Drink
by Mary M. Hale

F. was 18 months of age and had a past medical history of asthma. He was admitted to the pediatric unit this time with a cough, increasing temperature, an ear ache, and a runny nose of 2 days' duration.

His shortness of breath worsened overnight, requiring oxygen therapy. His parents had left him alone for the night. His birth history was that he had a 3-week stay in our NICU with increasing respiratory difficulty at 37 weeks of gestation. His permanent residence was with his great-grandmother, father, and mother. His dad was involved in his support and care. His diagnosis was "Group A hemolytic strep."

His physical environment included a bubble-top crib, side rails, and isolation. As we all know, familiar sights and sounds have a comforting effect on toddlers. He certainly knew how to wave "bye-bye" and shake his head, "No." His attention span was short with a preference for his own toys, which his parents had forgotten in their rush to provide medical care for their son. Besides the physiological stress of his multiple problems, he also had the separation from his parents, as well as the inappropriate stimuli of the various tests during his admission. He was refusing everything, including all fluids.

Then we had an idea about using something from the comfort basket, a diversional item often used with pain medications to bring comfort to a child. Should we choose a toy or perhaps something to persuade him to drink? We had small water canteens shaped like houses, airplanes, and stars. We tried putting apple juice in the airplane-shaped canteen, played with the airplane and the child for awhile, and left the canteen in the crib. He continued to cry as we closed the isolation door.

I stood outside the door and watched. The TV was on with its diversional music. He explored the objects in his bed by banging, throwing, and dropping them, then he tasted them. When he came to the airplane, he looked at it and drank from the plastic straw attached to it. At about 2 a.m. the security officer called to say that his parents were in the lobby and wanted to come and visit him. Since he had been asleep when they left at 9 p.m., they were surprised by all the activity since they left. They had returned with his favorite teddy bear and found him holding his "dee-dee," a sound that he had developed related to his drink. Toddlers do not misbehave on purpose. They understand "No," but still need us to direct their attention to another more appropriate activity. The successful recovery of F. can be directly attributed to his oxygen therapy, antibiotic, pain medication, and diversional activity, along with a caring, loving family and nursing staff who utilized a firm, direct approach with him. When we said goodbye to F. he held as tightly to us as he did to his parents, and cheered us all by saying "dee-dee". We all miss him.

George's story is different. It illustrates how the comfort basket provides comfort in the simplest form. Keeping warm is an important way to alleviate pain and George, at 12 days old, definitely needed warmth.

PROVIDING COMFORT THROUGH WARMTH
by Mary M. Hale

Christmas is a season when little infants sometimes have cold feet. George was in the hospital and on the day of his circumcision he was a little irritable. George had been transferred from the neonatal intensive care unit to the pediatric unit to complete his 14 day course of antibiotic therapy for meningitis. When I took care of George, he was 12 days old. "Keep the infant free from pain and keep him warm," was the order. But sometimes we forget the infant's feet. My mother used to teach me when I was a child that if your feet are warm, your whole body is warm.

We know that pain is whatever the child says it is or, in the case of an infant, whatever the nurse observes, especially if a quiet facial expression of physical distress is seen. The facial expression is often the most consistent behavioral indicator of pain in infants. Finding warm Christmas socks for George in the comfort basket was not unusual. They are often in great supply around the holidays. Infant sizes are no problem. We just pull them all the way up, as high as they'll go. One common denominator among all the infants, from the preemies on up, is the sigh of contentment after their warm Christmas socks are on and their pain medication is given.

A common theme is apparent in the stories told here: Nurses "going the extra mile" to make life better for the children in their care. These nurses were creative in the ways they managed childhood pain and discomfort. Many children are too young or otherwise unable to express their needs and fears. The nurse must be particularly astute in order to catch their nonverbal pain clues. They also rely on families, when available, to report signs of pain in their children. This is no small task.

Nurses need to console and cheer, brighten, and cajole as they comfort. In a moment's notice they must be prepared to devise an individualized approach to alleviate a child's pain, fear, and anxiety. Being artists or clowns, serious or flaky, or developing approaches like the comfort basket, nurses make a difference in the lives of children who are in pain. One very special quote written by Morse (1996) summarizes the comfort work of nurses:

> Comfort involves the nurse's use of intuition and empathetic responses. It involves using all available nursing knowledge. Comforting draws upon clinical knowledge and experience. It involves understanding theory and recognizing the normal course of such abstract concepts as hoping, developing trust, or suffering. And providing comfort includes caring not only for the patient but caring for the parent within the context of his or her life, work, and family (p. 6).

REFERENCES

Morse, J. M. (1996). The science of comforting. Reflections, 22(4), 6-7.

ADDITIONAL READINGS

Betz, C. L. (1998). Pain in children: Progress and challenges. Journal of Pediatric Nursing, 13(1), 1.

Boughton, K. et al. (1998). Impact of research on pediatric pain assessment and outcomes. Pediatric Nursing, 24(1), 31-35.

Carlson, K. L. (1998). Selected resources on pediatric pain. Journal of Pediatric Nursing, 13(1), 64-66.

Maikler, V. E. (1998). Pharmacologic pain management in children: A review of intervention research. Journal of Pediatric Nursing, 13(1), 3-14.

McCarthy, A. M. , Cool, V. A. , & Hanrahan, K. (1998). Cognitive behavioral interventions for children during painful procedures: Research challenges and program development. Journal of Pediatric Nursing, 13(1), 55-63.

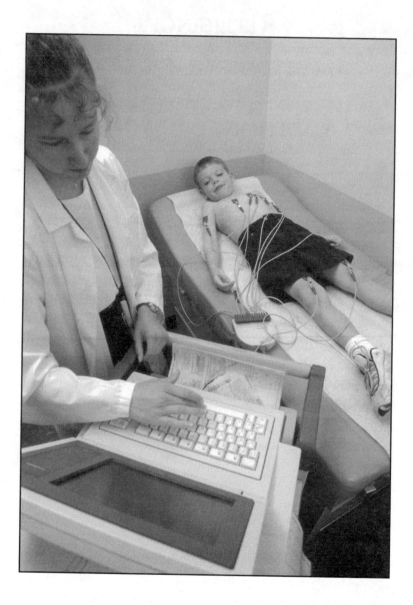

CHAPTER 6

Competence: Having Theoretical and Technical Know-How

It is clear from the stories in the previous chapters that nurse work involves sensitive and humanistic approaches. However, it would be a huge omission not to mention the knowledge and technical skill it takes to perform nurse work in the world of healthcare today. Nurses must have manual dexterity, be quick to respond, know when to act and know if the treatment/procedure is appropriate. This means the nurse must be technically and theoretically competent.

Competence means being able to function according to standards; to have the qualities to make decisions and be responsible for them (McGraw-Hill Nursing Dictionary, 1989). Nurses must be able to accurately assess, plan for short- and long-term goals, choose the correct action, and evaluate what they have done all while being sensitive to the patient's unique qualities. Completing these processes requires an incredible body of knowledge from both the behavioral, social, and the natural and biological sciences (biology, chemistry, anatomy and physiology, microbiology), and the arts (mathematics, literature, languages, and philosophy). Day-to-day job requirements include understanding complex lab data, analyzing symptoms that signal a rapidly changing condition, and intervening skillfully and on time. Competence also includes promoting health, decreasing risks, and preventing disease.

Nurses must be skilled teachers, helping patients understand their conditions and therapies so they can follow through with the protocols once the critical period is over. They must also be alert to life-threatening drug reactions or symptoms that warrant immediate assistance and teach these skills to the patient. Keeping current, given the many technical advancements and new drug discoveries, is a full-time job in itself.

A core competency for every nurse is keeping the patient hopeful, free of anxiety, and ready to accept the inevitable, whether it be a positive outcome or otherwise. Thus managing patient care includes physiological, psychological, and social dimensions that are constantly changing. Like a kaleidoscope, nurse work changes every moment requiring the know-how to respond quickly. The following scenario serves as an example of this kind of multifaceted competence.

CHANGING REQUIREMENTS
by Mary Jane K. DiMattio

Mr. K. had open-heart surgery. He was recovering without incident until one day he experienced a rapid, irregular heart beat. After speaking with the physician on the telephone, I administered a medication through Mr. K's. intravenous device. Because he had never had the medication before, I explained the action of the medication to him, and stayed with him to watch his heart monitor and to take his blood pressure.

After several minutes, Mr. K's. heart rate returned to normal but the rhythm was still irregular. I told him to remain in bed. I left the room and returned a few minutes later to find him standing at the side of his bed. When I asked if something was wrong, he smiled and said, "Oh, I'm okay, I just feel a little itchy," and he waved to indicate I need not be concerned about him. I was concerned, however, and went into the room to examine him. The palms of Mr. K's hands were pink, and he had a fine rash on his upper back. I quickly called out to another nurse and asked him to call the medical resident to see Mr. K. immediately. I brought emergency medications to Mr. K's room.

By now, Mr. K. was looking very frightened. I calmly explained to him that he might be experiencing an allergic reaction to the heart medication. I reassured him that I would obtain the proper treatment. Mr. K. was now very itchy and his face was beginning to swell. As soon as the physician saw Mr. K. and heard my assessment, he ordered two medications for allergic reaction to be given immediately. Within minutes, Mr. K. began to experience relief from the itching, and the swelling subsided.

Competence must always include the ability to relate to the patient in a meaningful way. Even when the prognosis is not good, the nurse must be able to use interpersonal and communication skills to help the patient remain calm and ready to accept death. While the activities may seem simple, knowing when and what to say is crucial.

COMPETENCE AND CARING
by Kathy J. Bolka

Mr. M. was one of those patients who just touches your heart a little differently. Mr. M. had emphysema and was waiting to have an operation to help improve his respiratory status. I knew a lot about him. I knew what he liked to talk about and what he feared. I had taken care of Mr. M. for a few weeks, and he was being discharged to another hospital to have the operation. I couldn't let him go without wishing him well. I made him a "good luck" card with a piece of paper and some magic markers and had everyone on staff sign it. I kissed him on the cheek, gave him his card, and made him and his wife promise they would call us with a complete report.

A week passed. The phone rang on Wednesday night. It was the ER with a report on an admission we were getting. It was Mr. M. "How did the surgery go?" I asked. He answered, "I didn't have the operation." He had pneumonia and the operation was postponed until he got better. Unfortunately, over the next few weeks, Mr. M's condition deteriorated. I spoke with his pulmonary doctor and knew that Mr. M. wasn't going to have an operation. Mr. M. was told the news as well.

He called me to his room about 15 minutes before my shift was over. When I got there I found him crying. He told me he was afraid. I held his hand and talked to him for awhile and then said goodnight. As the days passed, his breathing became even more labored. It was only a matter of time and Mr. M. knew it. Before I left that Friday night, I stopped in his room to say goodnight. I leaned over his bed, kissed his cheek and whispered in his ear, "Don't be afraid." He answered softly, "Kathy, I'm not afraid anymore. I'm tired and I'm ready."

On Saturday, my friend called to tell me that Mr. M. had died. I remember crying and then smiling because I knew that he wasn't suffering anymore. Mrs. M. called me a few days later and thanked me for my care. She wanted to tell me that she put the card I made in his casket with him because it meant so much to him.

I love being a nurse. It's hard work and we don't always get the thanks or recognition we deserve. However, I am fortunate enough to have my story to tell and when the days are really tough, I find myself thinking of Mr. M. and smiling.

A competent nurse must also use knowledge from the arts to care for patients. Since language is an important part of our lives, being able to speak the language of the patient is a great asset for the nurse. It not only allows for clear communication but conveys that the nurse is sensitive to the patient's needs.

SHOWING CULTURAL COMPETENCE
by Eileen M. Alexy

My most memorable clinical experience was with a patient I will call Marie and her family. I work on a unit with a population of patients age 65 and over who are diagnosed with dementia and depression.

Marie was a 75-year-old woman with dementia who only spoke Italian. She was brought to our unit because she had stopped eating and had become physically aggressive with her family caregivers. She had been living alone in a house next door to her son. The family had removed the stove and had the gas turned off in an effort to protect her because she left the burners turned on due to her "forgetfulness." Family members brought her meals, but because she had begun to wander, the family locked her in the house.

When Marie arrived on our unit she spoke only Italian. Her son and grandchildren served as interpreters because no one on our unit was fluent in Italian. Marie's affect changed dramatically when the staff attempted to toilet her. She became physically aggressive, hitting and scratching. I quickly learned the Italian words for toileting from her son, and I intervened by stroking her face and explaining what we were doing. She looked at me, smiled, held my hand and quickly calmed down. When the task was completed, Marie asked my name. Through her son, I learned the closest thing in Italian to Eileen was Eleanora. We quickly became friends. When I came to work each day and Marie saw me, her face would light up and she would yell "Eleanora, Eleanora."

Beyond language barriers and behavior issues, the greatest challenge was educating and supporting the family. I have to say as a nurse, my most memorable experiences are with both patients and their families. I am given the opportunity to support and educate all parties involved, and in the process I learn a lot about myself, and a little conversational Italian.

Sometimes patients seek healthcare not knowing there is something seriously wrong. During an assessment of the patient, the nurse may find clues to a serious condition and must be ready to proceed accordingly and help the patient accept the bad news. In the following story, nurse Helen was astute at picking up these kinds of clues and knew what to do so her patient received the proper treatment. This kind of competence is based on knowing what these clues mean and what should occur. Note how she prepares the patient for what he can expect in the future as a result of the diagnosis. This nurse behavior is called anticipatory guidance and is so important to the future health of a patient.

ASSESSING WITH COMPETENCE
by Helen A. Rigez

He was a young veteran, only 36-years-old, who came to my clinic for the first time. He had a job, a family, children he was proud of, and every bit the productive individual with all that life has to offer.

His decision to come for healthcare was related more to the wife's urging then his own "not feeling just right." Delving into his history and present symptomology, I, too, had this "feeling." As I completed the appropriate initial questionnaire and health promotion screening, I silently reviewed his background.

We discussed the routine tests and perfunctory explanation of primary care, and the meaning of advance directives. All too well, I knew where I was headed with this veteran. With an immediate family history of kidney disease, it was obvious he needed a work-up to see how far the disease had progressed.

Ordering the routine lab work, I called the nephrologist with my suspicions to alert him of this patient's imminent need for his services. He suggested I order a CT scan of the abdomen/kidney region. This was forwarded to the clerk for scheduling.

However, as luck would have it, the CT machine "was down" temporarily. I personally went to radiology and called in a favor. The patient was scheduled first thing Monday morning, giving the patient time to discuss issues, which were both personal and medical, with his family.

Following the CT scan and a subsequent physician appointment, the veteran came to see me with his father. It was evident upon review of all the data that he carried the genetic disorder to which his mother had succumbed while he was a teenager. While the patient was prepared for immediate dialysis, he kept me up-to-date on the projected treatment plan and the possibility of a kidney transplant from a relative.

Within one week, life had changed. This man's perspective on life had sharpened. I marveled at the knowledge I had accrued over the years to enable me to give this person a chance for a future. Life would never be the same for both of us. I thank God every moment for the knowledge I have which enabled me to help this man.

Accurate assessments are the key to proper treatment. In this next story, the nurse demonstrates the skill it takes to make an accurate assessment. Please note that these are independent nurse assessments and that physicians depend on the nurse's competence in making the correct assessment.

ASSESSING WITH CRITICAL ACCURACY
by Andrea Stetson

About a year ago, I took care of a patient who had recently had bypass surgery. She was transferred in stable condition from the step down unit the previous day. During my routine assessment, I noticed that her entire thigh was extremely edematous, (swelling due to a collection of fluid) and was firm and tender to the touch. Her suture lines were oozing pink-tinged fluid and her blood pressure was low. Her heart rate was elevated, and her level of consciousness was decreased. I promptly called the surgical resident who came to the bedside. She was on a Heparin (a blood thinner) and her lab results revealed that her clotting time was high. She had developed a large hematoma and was bleeding internally at her surgical site. We quickly gave her two units of fresh frozen plasma. She was transferred to the step down unit for closer monitoring. If her condition had not been noticed, the outcome would have been more serious. Astute assessment is just one of the many skills an RN must have and be able to initiate.

Timing is an important aspect of competent nurse work. Knowing the right time to act, speak, and mobilize resources is an essential aspect of being competent. Taking the time to listen, hear concerns, and teach patients about their healthcare can make an important difference in the way the patient's treatment progresses. Finding time to visit a patient transferred to another hospital and making the time to provide one-to-one care are examples of how important timing can be. A back rub, flowers or a cup of tea can make a big difference in the patient's healing.

CARING BY THE GIFT OF PRIVACY
by Antoinette Barto

I cared for a 55-year-old man with a severe cardiac condition and lung disease. "Joe, can I get anything for you?" I asked. "How about a new heart and lungs?" he responded. He was always pleasant, always joking. He visited our telemetry unit often and became well known to all of us. His wife and children (including a 10-year-old) visited nightly.

Joe was getting worse and his wife knew it. They discussed options and he wanted to be a DNR (do not resuscitate). Several days passed and his status drastically deteriorated. It was the end of my 3 to 11 shift and I knew that Joe would die during the night and his wife knew it too. Allowing them the privacy and decency that they needed to say goodbye was something I will never forget. Joe was getting pain medication, yet was still awake and communicative. Our goal was to make this time what they wanted it to be. I think we did that by providing comfort and time with the family.

I, too, said goodbye to Joe that evening. I left, got in my car, turned on the radio and "Spirit in the Sky" was playing. I know Joe was telling me something. Every time I hear that song, I think of him.

Learning How to be There
by Mary Mariani

I was 18 years old, and starting my initial fall rotation as a junior nursing student in San Francisco. It was a Saturday morning and I had at least three patients to care for. I don't recall the other two, but the third patient was R.S.

After giving a.m. care before breakfast, I began attending to the routine needs of my three patients. About 9:00 a.m., R.S. became pale and shaky and developed hypotension (a dropped blood pressure). I hardly left her bedside. After the first hour of this intensive care, the supervisor reassigned my other patients. I began 1:1 care at her bedside.

R.S. was weak and responsive throughout the day. I worked closely with the senior surgical resident to keep up with her intensive need for care, such as IV fluids, nasogastric irrigations, lab work, blood transfusions, pain medication, spiritual needs, and communications with her family. R.S. went to the OR and came back in stable condition. Thereafter, her recovery was uneventful. She returned home within 10 days.

How I happened to be there with her at the right time, I will never know. I could have been bathing another patient and not heard her buzzer, but that is not how it happened. She was the first patient I cared for who suffered an acutely critical event. I was able to remain with her providing her with the care she needed. I subsequently learned how to be there for the hundreds or thousands of other patients I have cared for in my 40-year career. Thank you, R.S.

Helping to Achieve Peaceful Closure
by Anonymous

Several years ago, while working as a medical-surgical nurse on a tertiary care unit, I was assigned an elderly female patient who was dying of lung cancer. Her husband was constantly at the bedside and was deeply in love with his wife of 58 years. He searched for ways to help her, going out for her favorite snack in the middle of the night and keeping her comfortable. That morning she was near death and he seemed at a loss. Hearing and seeing how close they were, I suggested he sit down next to her, hold her hand, and just reminisce about their life together, telling her all he wanted to say to her.

She was a "no-resusciatation" and I took care that they wouldn't be disturbed. She was unconscious by that time. He asked if she would hear him. I explained that often dying persons can hear what is being said, even though they cannot respond. He spent 3 hours with her talking and reminiscing. After she died, he said, "You can't know what a great gift you gave us. I talked all about our life together. You helped us to die in love." And then he hugged me.

GOING THE EXTRA MILE
by Amanda Bulette Coakley

Many years ago when I was a staff nurse working on an orthopedic unit, I had the experience of caring for a young man whose name was Larry. He had been in a terrible accident and was a patient on our unit for 12 weeks. He was receiving antibiotics after one surgery and was awaiting bone-graft surgery. Larry was about 100 miles away from home, which meant his family would usually visit on weekends and sometimes only every other weekend since one of his parents worked on weekends. He was a quiet, lonely young man. It appeared as if his parents did not have much money so the nurses on the unit arranged for his TV to be turned on so he could at least watch television. Sometimes when I worked on the weekends, I would play cards with him and talk with him about his family and friends. We established a very good rapport and I became his primary nurse.

As his bone infection was healing it was determined that he could have the bone-graft surgery. Unfortunately, it was close to Christmas and all the OR time was booked so his surgeon could not arrange for him to have his surgery at the hospital where I worked. However, his surgeon had operating privileges at another hospital, and decided to transfer Larry there for his surgery on Dec. 23rd and then transfer him back to the hospital where I worked on Christmas day for his recovery period. He was lonely and did not know anyone at the new hospital. After I finished work that day, I went to visit Larry and gave him money to have his TV turned on. I was thinking about how lonely he was and how difficult it must be to be in the hospital at Christmas. I was especially glad to see him and to tell him how much everyone on the unit was looking forward to his return on Christmas day.

Sadly, Larry never returned on Christmas because he died of a pulmonary embolism in the Operating Room on Dec. 23rd. I attended his funeral with a small group of nurses from the unit and was told by his family how much he thought of me. Every Christmas, I think of Larry and that trip to take him money. It was a snowy day and with everything I had to do to get ready for Christmas, I would have preferred not going, yet something told me to go. I am glad that I am a nurse and a person he could talk with comfortably. I am very glad that I went and helped him that one last time before he died.

Another aspect of competence is helping patients understand their health conditions. In the following scenario, telling the patient about her condition gave her information she needed so she could help the physician make the proper diagnosis. Keeping patients informed is a great asset to the plan of care.

LISTENING TO THE PATIENT
by Anonymous

As a medical-surgical nurse I see a variety of patient problems. Within this large urban teaching hospital, patients are seen by many medical students, residents, and staff physicians. A 45-year-old woman was a patient of mine. She had been admitted 3 days earlier with coagulation abnormalities of unknown origin. Unable to diagnose her problem, the doctors treated potential clotting with a medication, which was increased daily.

Her blood clotting time was not rising, as would normally be expected. I went in to see my patient on initial rounds and sat down to talk with her. She was an intelligent, conversant woman who was concerned about her illness. It seemed as though she was confused about what was being done to her, and why.

She saw doctors come in and out, never talking to her, just to each other. I explained to her that her blood coagulation level was not rising in response to her medication. I told her everything I knew about her case, reviewing her chart with her. She said this was the first time anyone had taken the time to discuss her illness, "You know, I was told years ago that I have a rare blood-factor deficiency. Could that be contributing to the problem?" I immediately notified the doctor who then ordered a factor analysis and the problem was found. Treatment was changed accordingly, the patient responded, and was released 2 days later.

Competent nurses are always learning. They not only attend classes and pursue advanced academic degrees, but they learn from each nursing experience. They often find themselves learning during each patient encounter. Sometimes what they learn is not what they expected to learn. Frequent shifts in the patients' conditions and in what happens in their families demands the nurse respond accordingly.

HELPING HEAL EMOTIONALLY
by Amy Gillan

She was in extreme pain, especially in her left flank area, accompanied by extreme nausea and even vomiting. It seemed obvious that Nancy had a left kidney stone, but when the tests for kidney stones and other tests turned out to be negative, the doctors were puzzled. What then was the cause of this pain? During these days of pondering for some type of explanation, the son, daughter, and husband of Nancy had many questions. This family was very anxious. I would remain calm and explain to them what was found from the tests and told them that it sometimes takes time and patience to finally arrive at a diagnosis.

To my surprise, the next day it was revealed the patient had developed shingles on her left flank area, which eventually led to a full-blown rash covering not only her left flank but also the front of her abdomen. At last a diagnosis to ease the anxiety, but an alteration in body image had set in.

While Nancy was recovering, doom's day occurred. She learned that her husband had died of a sudden heart attack while driving his car that morning. I gave Nancy, as well as her son and daughter, emotional support. The family and I had developed a close rapport and they trusted me by sharing their feelings and worries. I discussed with them the funeral arrangements as well as their feelings of guilt and anger. Nancy felt guilty, as if she caused her husband's death. "If only we didn't have the problems we had and if only I weren't sick, perhaps this would not have happened."

December 24th came and Nancy was finally ready for discharge. I called social service for home care, as this was a factor in her discharge as well as the need for home healthcare in order to help around the house with her husband gone. She tapped me on the shoulder and gave me cookies to give to the nurses and then winked at me and said "this is for you" and gave me a card. She also gave me a hug and a kiss.

I had helped to heal her emotionally, just as the quote, "Nursing is not only a science but an art" suggests. I think this situation exemplifies that statement.

COMPETENCE AND LEARNING
by Jennifer Novobilski

We do so much as nurses. The reason I entered this profession was to help people and one of the best feelings is when your patient's eyes light up when you walk into the room. I remember one patient, whose blood analyses were not good. The physicians were working him up for a possible gastro-intestinal bleed, but his special studies and diagnostic procedures were negative. I had just started a blood transfusion when the patient started complaining of chills and was shaking violently. I clamped the tubing and followed the protocol for the situation.

The patient was scared, not knowing what was happening. It turned out he needed a blood warmer. I took the time to explain to the patient why he felt the way he did and comforted him regarding his condition. The next day, he needed another transfusion and was very nervous about it. But again, I explained about the warmer and the importance of the transfusion. I checked on the patient frequently and everything turned out fine. After the transfusions the patient stated "The red blood count was not my biggest concern, it was the fact that I didn't know what was wrong with me."

The compliments I received have shown me I had an impact on this patient's life. Talking with this patient, sitting on the edge of his bed and taking his hand demonstrated how much I cared. Being able to solve problems and seeing that he was safe demonstrated competency.

I've been an RN for approximately 9 months. The job is difficult at times, but validation like this makes it all worthwhile.

CARING WITH CONSISTENCY
by Sue Idczak

In my senior year of nursing school at a large university, I was taught theory in psychiatric nursing by a psychiatrist, Dr. O. He was an excellent lecturer and although I did not clinically enjoy psychiatric nursing, my professor was such a good teacher that I enjoyed the lectures. The fall semester ended and I moved on to my next rotation, advanced nursing/leadership.

I worked as a student nurse in a cardiac step-down unit through my senior year, and took my first job as an RN in the same unit. Dr. O. had a massive heart attack that late winter/early spring and I was his student nurse several times during his hospitalization.

Through the next 20 years of my practice, our professional paths continued to cross. For example, I worked in an electro-physiology lab and Dr. O. had several more arrhythmia episodes which required several stays in the same step down unit due to Congestive Heart Failure. We developed a strong bond of trust. When he would see me in the hospital cafeteria or in the corridors he would stop and inform me about how he was doing or ask for a "hallway consult."

Eventually he became a candidate for a heart transplant. Ironically I was the cardiac transplant coordinator by this time and was involved in his work-up, the transplant itself, and follow-up care.

I left my position 4 years ago to marry and move out of state but Dr. O. still is near and dear to my heart. Some of my beliefs as a professional nurse include the ability to provide a trusting, supportive, caring role and to be a constant source of reference for the patients in the interactions they have in their healthcare.

Our profession is wonderful. Not only do we give a great deal of ourselves to our patients, but the patients return far more than we ever give to any of them. I could write story after story but Dr. O's. story represents one of my favorite.

The next story could be seen as humorous. But for the nurse who cared for the patient, it was a discovery that helped her see the importance of what the patient wants and deems is an issue. Competent nurses are able to follow the care plan and to alter it when the patient presents new information.

GOING WITH THE PATIENT'S PRIORITIES
by Anonymous

This particular story sticks out in my mind because it happened rather recently. I was taking care of a female patient hospitalized for a variety of cardiac problems, including undergoing a cardiac catheterization and pacemaker insertion. She had been hospitalized at another institution for about a week prior to being transferred to my facility. She was post-heart attack and was to have two very critical procedures performed on her heart, but her heart was the least of her worries.

All this patient could focus on was moving her bowels, because she hadn't done so for a week. For me, this was an easily solved problem. After a little medication and a suppository, my patient's biggest problem in her mind was resolved. She proceeded to have an uneventful hospital course, undergoing the procedures for which she was transferred about 2 weeks later. I received a letter from this patient on the nursing unit stating how I was her "savior" and how she couldn't have made it through her hospitalization without me.

Receiving the letter struck me in a very humorous way, seeing that I'm usually not so cordially thanked for assisting people with their bowel dilemmas. But, with this particular woman, there was nothing more important I could have taken care of!

PROVING COMPETENCE
by John J. Williams

After I had been an RN for about 1 year, I worked in an outpatient dialysis unit. We treated about 20 patients per shift. I worked the afternoon shift from 2 p.m. to 10 p.m.

One day, a patient, I'll call M.S., went into cardiac arrest while on dialysis. The technician immediately checked her pulse and found none. He called for a nurse and we took the patient off the machine and placed her on the floor and immediately started CPR. I gave the patient mouth-to-mouth while the technician did the compressions. After a couple of minutes, the patient's heart resumed pumping and she regained consciousness. She was taken to the hospital by ambulance and resumed dialysis the following week.

Dialysis patients don't like new people placing them on dialysis machines. Before I gave CPR to M.S., patients didn't particularly like me to put them on the machine. But after I administered CPR to M.S., they all wanted me to do it. I had proved to them I was competent!

Competent nurses are not rare. In fact, they are everywhere doing high quality nurse work. The stories in this chapter exemplify the many aspects of competent care, including effective communication, expert assessments, right timing, creative interventions, patient teaching, continuous learning and being recognized as competent. There are endless stories like the ones in this chapter that demonstrate the quality of care provided by competent nurses around the globe. These stories are but a small sample of what nurses are educated to do and how well they perform.

ADDITIONAL READINGS

Bellack, J. & O'Neil, E. H. (2000). Recreating nursing practice for a new century. Nursing and Healthcare perspectives, 21(1), 14-21.

Deaton, B. J. , Essenpreis, H. , & Simpson, K. R. (1998). Assessing competence: Meeting unique needs of nurses in small rural hospitals. AWHONN Lifelines, 2(5), 33-37.

Hewlett, P. O. , & Eichelberger, L. W. (1999). Creating academic/service partnerships through nursing competency models. Journal of Nursing Education, 38(7), 295-97.

Nolan, P. (1998). Competencies drive decision-making. Nursing Management, 29(3), 27-29.

Yoder-Wise, P.S. (1999). Leading through competence. Journal of Continuing Education, 30(5), 198.

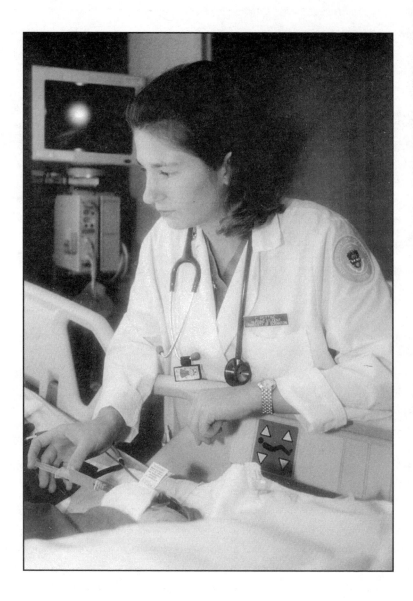

CHAPTER 7

Critical Thinking: A Core Competency

The ideal critical thinker is inquisitive, well informed, open-minded, flexible, prudent in making judgments, willing to reconsider, orderly in complex matters, diligent in seeking information, focused on inquiry, and persistent in seeking results which are as precise as the subject and circumstances permit (American Philosophical Association, 1990).

All nurses must make critical independent decisions since they are licensed practitioners held accountable by the law for their actions. Nurses in critical care and cardiac care units, however, often have more risky decisions to make because of the acuity of the patients' conditions and the protocols established for their care. These nurses must make countless, difficult, and sometimes life-threatening decisions, often when no one is available for validation or help. Even when colleagues are near, they practice independent of supervision or physician direction much of the time.

With expedience, the nurse must analyze lab data, recognize subtle changes in the patient's condition, and adjust the appropriate medications. Astute assessment and accurate interventions are necessary as they hastily assemble equipment and implement treatments and protocols. These nurses must be quick on their feet, alert, and ready to begin emergency protocols independently. Often, time is not on their side.

Nurses who function in critical and cardiac care units usually have advanced education in topics such as hemo-dynamics, arrhythmia detection, and advanced life support. The ability to judge treatments in terms of efficacy and safety is often a major part of their job. A poor deci-sion could mean a patient's condition would worsen. The wrong deci-sion could mean the patient's life would be at risk.

While critical and cardiac care nurses work independently and must make critical decisions, they are also a part of a healthcare team. They collaborate with physicians; respiratory, occupational, and physical ther-apists; radiologists; and social workers. In 1993, Maria Chiara conduct-ed a qualitative analysis of what nursing means to nurses and what val-ues and expectations nurses bring to their work. She found that nurses wanted the opportunity to make a difference in people's lives and to accept the challenge of being patients' advocates. Several of the nurses said that the most rewarding aspects of their careers were working with other members of the healthcare team. Teamwork, they said, brought lasting bonds of friendship and strong support for their contributions.

Experience is a fundamental expectation for nurses who work in crit-ical and cardiac care areas. Most have had years of experience as staff nurses before working in the specialized area of critical care. They have had good supervision, quality mentors and as a result they are experts in their area of care.

Nurses who function in critical and cardiac care units are gifted in special ways. Some provide great spiritual comfort. Others are ingenious with high-tech equipment. Still others possess talent in working with chil-dren or the elderly. All must be effective communicators and teachers to help patients learn what to expect so they can make informed decisions.

The following story told by nurse Bob illustrates the scope of his activ-ities as a critical care and ER nurse. Note his ability to identify the real problem was partly due to his being a good listener and partly because he knew what to look for as a critical thinker.

SEEING THE CAUSE OF THE SYMPTOMS
by Bob Gaudreau

My first encounter with Paul was when I was working in a 12-bed ICU. Paul was on a breathing machine and had a diagnosis of "status asthmaticus." He had many previous hospitalizations because of his asthma and this was not his first intubation. He was a 55-year-old Korean War veteran, single, retired from the Army and had a second medical diagnosis of anxiety. During my 2-1/2 years in the ICU, Paul was intubated on two more occasions because of his asthma.

Because I worked the 7 p.m. to 7 a.m. shift, I never saw Paul extubated. He was extubated on the day shift, recovered quickly, and was transferred to a medical ward to continue treatments until time of discharge.

About 3 years later, I was reassigned to the Emergency Room to begin my new career. Soon after taking this new position Paul was brought in by ambulance in an acute asthmatic attack. What I saw in him was more than just having a difficult time breathing: He had a look of sheer terror on his face. He had a rapid heart beat, was breathing rapidly, was perspiring profusely, had a high blood pressure, and was shaking and in a state of severe emotional distress. And his speech rambled when he received his nebulizer treatments. I administered the usual drugs as outlined in his protocol, but Paul continued to get worse. He was breathing so fast that his energy reserves were expended quickly. Again, Paul was intubated and transferred to the ICU.

About 2 months later, Paul was brought in again on my shift with an acute asthma attack. Again, what impressed me was the look of terror on his face and, of course, he had the same clinical manifestations as before. This time while administering the drugs needed to reverse his condition, I was able to make sense of what Paul was "rambling" about. Nightmares! As his breathing became worse, I started focusing on his mental condition. With calmness and reassurance on my part Paul slowly calmed down and his breathing became less labored.

Paul began telling me a story of horror. During the Korean War, he was taken prisoner by the Chinese and North Koreans. What he endured over the next 18 months was absolute "hell." Paul described to me the torture that was inflicted upon him on an almost daily basis. Not only physical but, maybe more serious, psychological. The talking seemed to help Paul tremendously, and his breathing improved as he talked. After being with us for almost 2 hours, Paul was admitted to the medical ward for continuing treatments, and was not intubated. What transpired over the next 2-1/2 years between us was very special. Every time Paul had a relapse, I was on duty and helped him down from his "horrific" memories of Korea. On many occasions, Paul was able to go back home from the ER. Then on one occasion, Paul was hospitalized already intubated. We did what we could for him in the ER and he was transferred to our ICU.

Paul died about 48 hours later, finally getting the peace he so badly needed. What Paul endured over those years since the end of the Korean War is impossible to understand. I know my interactions, my "reading" of what Paul was saying, verbally and non-verbally, were significant in turning around the physical manifestations of his relived torture sessions. As I look back now and try to address what it was that I did for Paul, I would have to say that not only was it the drugs that worked, but more importantly it was the human contact and understanding of his needs during those times that was most important.

The importance of quick action based on an accurate assessment cannot be overemphasized. Patients' conditions can change momentarily, and without immediate action they could suffer dire outcomes.

CRITICAL THINKING DURING ASSESSMENT
by Eric Hokien

As I walk onto my unit in the morning, it is unclear what the day might hold for me. I am a registered nurse working in a multi-discipline, critical care unit at a Level II trauma center. The most quiet day can instantly turn into a fast-paced, run-and-scramble, life or death situation.

Working 12-hour shifts, I consistently worked several days in a row, so naturally I was assigned to the same patients until they left the unit. On one particular morning, I was caring for a gentleman who had been assigned to me for the past three days. He was involved in a motor vehicle accident suffering multiple rib fractures and internal injuries. He had been in the intensive care unit several days and was to be transferred from our unit to the surgical unit in a day or two.

The man had a left chest tube previously inserted into his chest because of a collapsed lung. He had also had his spleen removed because of injuries suffered in the crash. Hampered by the rib fractures and trauma to his chest, his transfer from the unit was delayed because of a poor respiratory status.

After receiving report, I assessed my patient. Having cared for him the last several days, I wasn't expecting to find anything out of the ordinary. However, on initial assessment, I found his heart rate was elevated, his breathing slightly labored, an oxygen saturation around 92 %, and breath sounds absent on his right side. An oxygen saturation of 92 % was not an immediate concern. His oxygen saturation readings had been running around 96 % the last several days. I immediately called the x-ray department for the chest film taken that morning. In addition, I called the trauma surgeon to update him on my findings and asked him to look at the x-ray film.

As it turned out, the diagnosis was a collapsed lung on the right side. I had established a good relationship with the family, so I informed them of the situation, and shared their disappointment that this setback would keep him in ICU longer. Later, after a chest tube was inserted, the man's wife and daughter said they had heard that it was my assessment that identified the problem. They thanked me.

I find it rewarding to apply my knowledge to my work, and on this particular day, I had the opportunity to see the reward of my nursing judgment from a different perspective, the perspective of the family.

Critical thinking often means the nurse must make inferences, which means determining what will happen if something is or is not done. The nurse in the following story, while doing all that could be done, knew it was not enough and that more was required. The nurse persistently alerted the physician knowing his diagnosis would provide the treatment that was needed.

BEING PERSISTENT
by Colleen Crossen Babinsky

As I look back on my nursing experience, one patient to whom I feel I made a difference was a male Caucasian diagnosed with a myocardial infarction (heart attack). It was around 3 a.m. when the cardiac monitor alarm showed third-degree heart block and a heart rate in the low 30s. Following our protocol, I administered 1 mg Atropine IV and the doctor was immediately notified. The patient converted to normal heart rhythm, however, he became very confused and belligerent. There was something unusual about his response. I called the doctor again, asking him to come into the hospital to evaluate the patient, but he couldn't come. I asked him for an urgent cardiology consult, but he said it was not necessary because he would be there as fast as he could get there. The patient then started having heart irregularities.

I called the doctor again. At 8 a.m. and after several phone calls, the doctor arrived to examine the patient. By this time, the patient was back into third-degree heart block and was confused, belligerent, had a low blood pressure and low blood oxygen saturation readings. He was put on a temporary external pacemaker, ventilator, and medication by IV.

I did everything possible to stabilize the patient. Being persistent about getting the doctor to come was the most important action I took. It has been my experience that nurses are the ones who are there and see the most and thus are the ones who actually save the patients' lives!

Critical thinking is an interactive reflective process based on a consideration of evidence in order to arrive at a purposeful judgement (Thiele, 1993). Nurse Maria understood this aspect of critical thinking as she determined what was happening to her patient, and later as she helped him and his family make a critical decision of their own.

RESPECTING THE PATIENT'S WISHES
by Maria Carlucci

I have had many experiences that have affected me both as a nurse and as a person. There is one that had an impact on me more than any other, even though it did not have a happy ending.

My patient, Bill, had come to see the doctor because of constipation. The work-up revealed a large colon tumor was causing an obstruction. The surgeons wanted to remove the tumor, but Bill did not want any surgery. He was a realistic person and knew there was a chance he could have a prolonged hospitalization without a prolonged life span. He decided to go through with it, though, because of his family.

The night before his surgery I went to look at him and, fortunately, went in at the right time. He had a small amount of bright red blood on his gown and I could see he was starting to hemorrhage. I called a code and everyone worked well together. We quickly inserted a breathing tube, and started an IV into his femoral vein so we would have central access for quick fluid replacement. We also placed a tube into his stomach so we could wash it out. He was stabilized and his family was called. They came within half an hour.

The doctor's plan was to take him to the radiology department, find the bleeding, and stop it. However, Bill was neurologically intact and able to communicate indicating, by nodding yes or no, that he did not want anything done and wanted to die in peace. I know it was a hard decision for his family because they loved him. He and his wife had been married for about 35 years. Together they decided to withhold all treatment and to let him go peacefully. He died quickly with his family around him.

The reason this has had such an impact on me is because I see so many patients whose lives are prolonged for months in agony. I admire the difficulty of the decision Bill's family made. There are many people who do not enforce their loved one's wishes so patients are put through pain until they die. I feel that people lose touch with what is best for their loved one and I respect Bill's family for honoring his wishes above their own! I also believe it is the nurse's job to see that the patient's wishes are known, particularly if they cannot speak for themselves.

The next scenario is about a nurse who diligently worked to save a patient's life. She knew she had to stay with the patient and do what was needed or he would die. Involving the family was a wise decision in two ways: it gave them something to do during the crisis and it gave her the help she needed when no one else was available. Expanding the choices when making a decision is an important aspect of critical thinking.

PERSEVERANCE FOR THE PATIENT
by K. DeLong

One day I received a patient who was having bloody vomiting and diarrhea. The doctor ordered iced water stomach washings until clear. It took approximately 45-60 minutes to stop the bleeding. After 10 minutes, the patient would begin vomiting blood again or have bloody stools. So I would resume the iced washings. To make a long story short, I ice washed the patient for 5 hours until the doctor showed up and took him to the ICU for cauterization of the bleeding ulcer.

The patient's family was at the bedside throughout all this time and even kept refilling the saline pail for me so I did not have to stop the washing for any period of time. Once the patient was stable in the ICU, the doctor returned to thank me and to tell me that I was the only reason the patient was still alive and doing well.

Frequently, nurses are thrust into situations that seem to have no apparent solutions. Rules, protocols, and other barriers make it seemingly impossible for the patient to receive the kind of attention that is desired. It takes a nurse who is a critical thinker to figure out how to make the system work. The next story illustrates how one nurse individualized the options so the patient and her family could stay together when there was so little time left for them as a family.

DOING THE IMPOSSIBLE BECAUSE IT IS ESSENTIAL
by Anonymous

I was asked by Dr. T., an obstetrician, if I could take a pregnant patient of his, S. L., who was hospitalized on the neurology unit, for a tour of the delivery suite. She had an inoperable brain tumor and was about to deliver her first baby. As I was pushing her through the unit I learned that she had recently been diagnosed after experiencing a number of symptoms. She and her husband were both in their 30s, had successful careers and were really excited about having a baby.

The disastrous news about the tumor and poor prognosis was hard to accept and chemotherapy was out of the question because of the baby. Surgical debridement to decrease the growth of the tumor and to buy more time was the only alternative which was the reason for her hospitalization at this time.

Baby E. L. was born by cesarean section at term and was normal in every way. S. L.'s focus was to enjoy the baby for the short time she had with her family. Plans were made for her to have a normal post delivery stay in the postpartum unit. Soon after the delivery S. L. began to experience symptoms again and needed further debridement of the tumor. However this posed many problems.

Neuro patients had to be housed on the neuro floor. Babies were not allowed to stay on that floor. Postpartum nurses couldn't take care of a "neuro" patient and dads were not allowed to remain past visiting no matter where the patient was located. S. L. would be hospitalized for a week or more and the baby would be ready for discharge in a few days. What could be done to help this family? I could not imagine the mother on the neuro floor, the baby in the nursery and the father not able to visit except during strict visiting hours. And who would take care of the baby when it was time for discharge?

I decided to risk the impossible and to see if I could unite this family. I made calls to Risk Management, talked with the neuro nurses and arranged for a semi-private room for S. L. and her husband. Baby. E. L. was discharged to the care of her parents. The dad was allowed to stay in the semi-private room with S. L. and the baby. They remained in the hospital for 2 weeks until S. L. was strong enough to return to her home. S. L. died two months later.

E. L. is about 15 years old now. I have kept in touch with the family over the years. Her dad called me on her last birthday to say hello and to thank me for what I did for them when E. L. was born. I feel so lucky to have been able to help them.

Many of the decisions that nurses make are the result of an analysis of very subtle data. The tone of voice, the body position, or the words not expressed give the nurse the information that is so vital for making the right decision. Nurse Katie's story illustrates how careful listening, watching, and the sensing of cues are important when a critical decision is made. It also demonstrates how nurses learn from the information they gain during a patient-nurse interaction.

SEEING THE NEED OF OTHERS
by Katie

I was taking care of a premature infant who weighed two pounds. He was 2 days old and on a ventilator. Even though we were feeding him small amounts of mom's breast milk, there was residual milk collecting in his stomach (which is common with premature infants).

Just as we had decided to cut back on the number of feedings, his mom arrived to feed him. She was told we would be holding his feedings until further notice. I waited for her to come into the unit to hold him but she did not show up. Suddenly I realized that she may need to talk so I went to see her. I found her crying and very upset. She told me that while feeding her infant she felt "connected" with him and I realized how much terminating the feeding had affected her ability to bond with him.

This experience gave me a renewed appreciation for the bonding between mom and baby. It helped me see the breast-feeding experience as more than nourishment for the baby.

Nurses who work outside of the hospital have many opportunities to function independently. In fact, most of their practice is accomplished alone. They enter the patient's home as a guest and visitor never really knowing what they may find. The usual protocols, rules, and resources are not in place. The next two stories demonstrate how nurses, whose areas of specialty include wound care, address and solve patient problems using critical thinking.

CRITICAL HOME VISITS
by Linda Wessel

Working as a wound, ostomy, and continence nurse, I am often called to manage a variety of wounds from pressure ulcers to complicated draining wounds with multiple drains. On one occasion, I was asked to visit a patient who had undergone surgery for carcinoma of the common bile duct. She was terminal and had fluid and bile pouring through several points on her long chest and abdominal incision. The family members caring for her were using towels to keep her dry. Every time she tried to sit up or roll over the bedding became soaked.

I gathered my supplies and drove to her home 45 miles away. When I entered the house, I saw a rather large lady in bed with folded towels to each of her sides and laundry baskets full of wet towels from the night. She said, "I've prayed that you would come and help me."

I applied a large wound drainage collector over the extensive incision and taught the family how to change it. The collector stayed on several days. The lady lived for two more days dry and comfortable surrounded by her family. I know I made a difference in the last days of her life.

MAKING CARE MANAGABLE FOR THE PATIENT
by Anonymous

I am a nurse who specializes in the care of wounds, ostomies and incontinence. I love my work because it is very rewarding to help others adjust and learn how to manage their therapies. One patient in particular comes to mind. She was a young woman who was also a nurse but on medical disability due to a chronic illness.

She called our home care agency in tears one day because she was going home from the hospital and was sure she could not manage her ostomy care. Due to her underlying illness and obesity, she had a severe yeast infection on her skin. Her stoma was recessed and separated at least 1/2 inch from her skin. She had been instructed to perform a very complex procedure for changing the ostomy pouch that was not working. My goal was to simplify the procedure and make it more effective. Over the next week this was accomplished. By acknowledging her frustration she gradually began to participate in her care. Soon she was changing the appliance herself and feeling much better about the situation. It was rewarding to hear the words, "I don't think I need you anymore."

A new role for the nurse, and one that is increasing in numbers, is the parish nurse. These nurses usually function through churches, helping the pastor and priest care for the physical, emotional, and spiritual needs of the community of parishioners. They function fairly autonomously providing wellness care, referrals for health problems, and programs that promote physical, emotional, and spiritual health. In the next scenario a parish nurse demonstrates how she used critical thinking to solve a crisis for a family. In her story, the scope of decision-making was holistic, including all members of the family.

PARISH NURSING
by Diane McCurdy Crooks

"Ummm, I think we might need some help here," stated Bob in his usual calm manner. This was the telephone call I received one warm spring afternoon from the father of an active two-year old and husband to a 34 year-old dental assistant named Judy. Living with this couple and their child was his 90 year old mother and her 95 year old sister. Both ladies had diminished mental abilities.

Earlier in the day Judy had fallen when her heel caught on the carpet. She was taken to a nearby walk-in clinic that was operated by the local hospital where she was given pain medication and told to return home and elevate her leg. No x-rays were taken. In the meantime her leg had swelled to 3 times its normal size and she was in a great deal of pain.

After obtaining specific details, such as insurance coverage, etc., I decided it was necessary for her to immediately be seen by an orthopedist. I called a friend and obtained the name of a qualified M.D. who might be able to see her. I arranged for Judy and Bob to be seen as soon as they could get there. Since Judy and Bob could not leave his mother and aunt alone, I arranged for a neighbor to stay with them until Bob and Judy returned.

When Judy and Bob reached the physician's office she was whisked into the examining room, x-rayed, and made comfortable. The x-rays revealed two fractures of two leg bones, but thankfully there was no need for surgery. When the doctor asked how she was referred to him, Judy said "my Parish Nurse made the referral."

Three months later she was back at her job and helping to take care of the "ladies" at home.

The stories in this chapter are a tribute to all the nurses who have the responsibility of making critical decisions. We acknowledge their contributions because, while others may be near, they often cannot seek consultation before action is taken. They must stand accountable for the outcomes of their judgments. They must take quick and decisive action. And then there are those nurses who are not close to others, who have few resources and must depend on themselves for the right answer or the most appropriate intervention. We pay tribute to all of them.

REFERENCES

American Philosophical Association. (1990). Critical thinking: A statement of expert consensus for purposes of educational assessment and instruction. The Delphi Report: Research findings and recommendations prepared for the committee on pre-college philosophy. (ERIC Document Reproduction Service No. ED 315-423).

Chiara, M. (1993). Making a difference: An ethnography of women's career motivations, values, and work satisfaction in nursing. (Dissertation). Department of Anthropology, Northwestern University.

Thiele, J. E. (1993, April). Application of research to teaching clinical decision making. Paper presented at the Western Institute of Nursing Conference, Seattle, WA.

ADDITIONAL READINGS

Facione, N. C. , Facione, P. A. , & Sanchez, C. A. (1994). Critical thinking disposition as a measure of competent clinical judgment: The development of the California critical thinking disposition inventory. Journal of Nursing Education, 3(8), 345-350.

Sullivan, E. J. (1987). Critical thinking, creativity, clinical performance, and achievements in RN students. Journal of Professional Nursing, 3(2), 118-128.

Walsh, G. M. , & Hardy, R. C. (1999). Dispositional differences in critical thinking related to gender and academic major. Journal of Nursing Education, 38(4), 149-155.

Watson, G. , & Glaser, E. M. (1980). Critical thinking appraisal manual. San Antonio, TX: The Psychological Association.

CHAPTER 8

Creativity: Innovative Ways to Meet Patient Needs

In the past, care in the home was provided by public health nurses. They had a caseload of several families to care for and kept an account of their progress. They taught families about nutrition, child-care, and ways to stay well. They did post-hospital care, newborn follow-up care, and made referrals as needed. Most of the care was wellness-based and anticipatory.

Today, people in their homes are cared for by a variety of nurses such as home care nurses, hospice nurses, parish nurses, public health nurses, and a variety of ancillary helpers directed by nurses. Patients are sicker and need complex therapies and close supervision. Almost anything that is provided in the hospital is also available in the home. Providing nursing care for people in their homes today is much more different than it was in the past. It is a very complex and demanding job that requires innovative and creative approaches. The nurse may arrive at any time of the day or night, provide sophisticated therapy, or teach and supervise the care provided by the family or the home care technician. There is often a need to improvise or be creative because the home is not like the hospital where resources are plentiful and arranged for efficient use.

Being resourceful is a prerequisite for providing nursing care in the home. Referrals must be made, which means the nurse must have a comprehensive understanding of the eligibility requirements of the health programs in the community. It also means the nurse must have an understanding of the reimbursement options of private and government insurance agencies. Frequently the nurse must get very creative in order to provide the care that is needed given these eligibility and reimbursement requirements.

This chapter is about the creative ways that nurses help patients cope with illness, manage chronic conditions, and die with dignity. The stories presented are about the strategies nurses use to help family caregivers provide nutrition, treatments, and medications their family member needs, as well as what they do themselves to improve the patient's condition. There are also stories about what nurses do in a variety of places, even when they are having fun with their own families.

WHERE THE REWARDS ARE
by Elaine Allegrucci

Throughout my 23 years in the nursing profession, I have worked the night shift, have worked in operating rooms, offices, private duty settings, and most recently home health. My experiences have been very extensive. I have had to "code" patients and watch them live, reattach amputated limbs, and agonize over the long suffering and subsequent death of my father.

I had assumed that saving a patient's life when he arrested in front of me was the most rewarding, yet devastating, event in my career until just this past week. While I was on call one evening and in the midst of several complicated crises, a family member of a dying patient called. This young woman was so overwhelmingly frightened by the presence of her dying mother in her home that she was in a state of panic. Crying and screaming, she attempted to get across to me her inability to cope with the situation despite the fact that other family members were present. Her fear was so real that I could picture through the phone the tears streaming down her face. I attempted to console her but my efforts were unsuccessful therefore, I explained that I would be there as soon as possible and that I was approximately 30 minutes away. "Please come quick! " were her parting words.

After handling a few more calls, I bolted to the car and battled the snow squalls until I reached the home. Inside, approximately 10 pairs of eyes stared at me as if I were an unwanted intruder. What a wrong impression I had at that moment. A woman led me down a long hall and into a quiet room where my patient lay, unconscious and agonizing over each breath. At the next moment, the young woman, who was approximately 30 years old, entered the room wearing that same expression I had pictured on the phone. Through the tears she threw her arms around me saying, "I'm so glad to see you!" It was as though I, a stranger, had come to "save the night." The patient required very little except comfort measures and some pain medications. Her daughter was the real reason I was there.

Within the next three hours, we became close personal friends. Slowly, each member of the family entered the room, getting closer and closer not only to each other but also to the dying patient, their mother, grandmother, sister, aunt. I then knew each family member's name and relationship and they knew me. We all shared experiences, good and bad, including in the conversation how it all related to the wonderfully loved and cherished dying woman in the bed. As the night shift nurse came in, we all realized we had lost track of time. The night nurse was the epitome of caring and within 5 minutes had the entire family "eating out of the palm of her hand." Because I was so concerned about this family I stayed another hour. As I left, the hugs and kisses were flowing.

The patient died the next morning. Two days later, I called the daughter. She was coping quite well at that point and said, "You were an angel come down from heaven when I needed you." That is why I am still in the profession fighting through all of the politics, unfair pay, and inhuman hours. In case anyone hasn't noticed, nurses are in it for the personal and spiritual rewards.

HELPING PATIENTS WITH PROGRESS
by Mark Loftus

One patient will always be part of my personal and professional life. U.V. was a 68-year-old married man with six children. He was admitted to the hospital with weakness in his lower extremities. He had gross motor movements of his lower extremities and fine motor movements of both upper extremities. He was diagnosed with Guillain-Barre' Syndrome (GBS). Eventually he lost all motor activity, and required complete nursing intervention. As the days turned to weeks, U.V. faced the possibility of being placed on a breathing machine due to the advancing muscle weakness. During his hospitalization, I had the opportunity to get to know U.V. fairly well. We would talk about sports and his grandchildren.

As the GBS advanced, I was able to prepare him for what could happen. I cared for him frequently, almost daily. The thing I remember most is the communication we had. I could just look at him and know what he needed and what to do for him. This was especially helpful when he was placed on the breathing machine. When I was not responsible for his care, his assigned nurse would often come to me to see what he was asking for.

I finally taught him to cough or try to trigger the ventilator to get our attention. U.V. was a patient in our unit approximately 50 days. There were evenings that I would try to spend more time with him than usual. We would watch football or just talk. He said he would like to be home for Christmas. I tried to be realistic with him by saying that it might be a long time before he returned home. I believe he appreciated the time I spent with him.

Having cared for him I was motivated to gather as much information as possible about GBS. U.V. was scheduled to transfer to a rehab center in central Pennsylvania. The day before he was to be transferred, he was weaned from the ventilator, but still had a tube in his trachea. When I approached him to say goodbye, I removed his hand splint and shook his hand. As I wished him well he looked at me with tears in his eyes and mouthed the words "Thank you for all you have done for me, and I will be back to see you."

As the weeks and months passed, I would get periodic information regarding his progress. At first, it was a slow recovery, but about 2 weeks before Christmas, I received word that he was going home, ambulating with a walker, and his breathing tube had been removed.

Creativity often means doing things that might seem silly. However, being creative means being inventive, original, and imaginative (Oxford Dictionary and Thesaurus, 1996). This can take many forms, as is the case in the following stories.

RECRUITING PETS IN HEALTHCARE
by Marie K. Cieslik

Nurse work is not what I expected it to be. I worried over procedures, treatments, and various skills. Over the years, I have found that, while the skills, procedures, and tasks are important, the real impact of my nursing is not what I did but how I did it. As a hospice nurse, I once visited with a man I will call Mr. A., who was in the final stages of lung disease. His wife of 50 years was his caregiver. Mr. and Mrs. A. had a troubled past with a long history of alcoholism and domestic turmoil.

Upon meeting Mrs. A. I immediately sensed her fear of losing Mr. A. and her mistrust of a medical system that was saying there was nothing more to offer them. My work was to convince her that a lot more could be done to increase Mr. A.'s comfort, lessen her anxiety and enrich their remaining days together. Her concerns were about medications, oxygen, and nutrition. My thoughts were about peace, tranquility, and simple pleasures. Finally, Mrs. A. allowed me to meet her husband.

I found a very ill, depressed individual whose only desire was to be left alone. He told me some of their problems but his major distress was not about his physical condition or his shortened life expectancy. Rather he was concerned about his lack of appetite, lack of interest in food and his wife's insistence on feeding him. This is not an unusual family dilemma since many believe if we can feed it we can fix it. In the course of the next few visits, I explained in every way possible the implications, complications, and emotional strain caused by insisting that a sick dying person eat three big meals a day. Not only did Mrs. A. adhere to the nutritional recommendations of multiple servings from each food group by preparing meals that would be fit for a body builder, but she also presented her husband with between meal snacks of fruit, milk, and doughnuts.

The wall between Mrs. A. and her reluctant husband became more solid with each passing day. She tried with all of her heart to understand why it was natural for Mr. A. not to want to eat, but she could not bring herself to modify the size of her offerings nor accept anything but an empty plate in return for her efforts.

I believe part of the art of nursing involves accepting people where they are and how they are. In my efforts to do this and also to truly advocate for my patient I decided to do the following. The family dog, Rocky, was a constant companion to Mr. A. Rocky loved to nap next to the oxygen concentrator beside Mr. A.'s bed. It turned out Rocky also had a hearty appetite and a sweet tooth, because she gratefully accepted everything Mr. A. offered from his tray. It was to be our secret, Mr. A.'s, Rocky's, and mine. I know that Mrs. A. was onto us, but we all chose not to discuss this sensitive issue. As weeks passed, Rocky expanded, but Mr. and Mrs. A. found a peaceful time in their lives that had evaded them for so long.

MAKING CONNECTIONS
by Sandra Granger

I was working in my first nursing position in an Air Force hospital in Anchorage, Alaska. I had graduated from a bachelor's program in nursing at age 33 while raising a family. We moved to Alaska immediately after graduation when my military husband was transferred to Anchorage.

The male surgical ward where I was assigned (as the only civilian nurse on the unit) had frequent veteran as well as active duty and retired military patients. In early January, an elderly gentleman was air-evacuated to us from one of the more remote locations in Alaska. He had been partying on New Year's Eve, was dropped off by a cab at his small cabin home, and when he attempted to get back into his cabin out of the bitter cold, he could not unlock the door; either he had lost the key or something wasn't working right. By the time he was discovered, he had suffered severe frostbite on both hands and feet.

The patient, I shall call him Bob, was with us on our 32-bed ward for many months while he had treatment for his frostbite injuries. As he was a colorful Irish storyteller, he became a favorite to both staff and other patients. During his stay we became friends, and he shared the story of how he ended up in Alaska.

At the end of World War II when Bob returned from Navy duty, he spent a few days with family and boarded a train, ending up in Alaska. He did not keep in touch with his family. He talked about his mother and how badly he felt that he never kept in touch with her. At that point, he did not know if she was alive or what had happened to his siblings. After several times of hearing bits and pieces of his story, I asked him if he would allow me to try to find his family. He agreed that I could make an attempt, but he didn't appear very positive that we might actually find someone after 30 years.

I started my search for a connection to Bob by writing a letter to the editor of the Grants Pass, Oregon, newspaper. My letter stated the family name and described the approximate time that Bob thought the family lived there. I explained that I was a nurse working with Bob and that he was trying to locate family. Bob left the hospital to go back to his Alaska community shortly after I had started my search. It wasn't very long before I started to receive mail in response to my letter. (How quickly all of this might have happened if e-mail and the Internet had been around then!)

I received the most wonderful letters from Bob's family. Letters from a brother and sister described their mother and how she loved to dress up on Sundays with her hat and gloves and go for a ride in the car. She had died at age 92. Bob's niece, a flight attendant, was working out of Anchorage; she called me after the correspondence about her uncle. Bob was physically not able to write due to the injuries to his hands. Friends in his remote hometown in Alaska wrote letters to his family for him, and they sent me copies of their letters as they described this long-lost brother to his siblings. The photo of Bob when he was a patient on our ward was printed in a veteran's magazine. His family was very pleased when I sent them the clipping from the magazine.

I have never forgotten how pleased I was when responses from Bob's family were received. Making a connection for him became very important for me. The lieutenant colonel head nurse of our unit frequently called me the ward social worker. I didn't mind; I enjoyed that extra part of my job. I still have the letters I received from Bob's family and friends and have enjoyed reading them again from time to time.

Like so many nursing interventions, being creative has many forms. Simple things like listening and sensing something is wrong can be creative because it is a strategy for reaching deeper and finding out what is really happening.

INTERVENING AS A SCHOOL NURSE
by Marilynn Doenges

I was a public health nurse when we were trying to carve out new territory for nurses as independent practitioners in the school setting. It was an exciting opportunity to provide physical and mental health education and care for students and adults.

However, in spite of our efforts to show the other professionals that we had much to offer them, it was difficult to break out of the stereotype of the nurse who takes temperatures, says whether children are really sick or are faking, and handle first aid tasks. Nevertheless, I found my role challenging and exciting.

The incident I want to share started with one of those small complaints that are so common to school nurses. Beth was a 12-year old who stopped in my office to ask about a small mark on her arm. I had seen her before with a similar minor concern, so I encouraged her to talk, sensing there was more than the expressed concern. It would have been easy to brush her off as avoiding class and send her on, but my intuition said it was important to listen to her. As we talked, she told me her 2-year-old sister had died two years ago of a brain tumor. As I listened I realized this young lady was feeling depressed and decided to make a home visit. I called her mother and arranged to see both Beth and her mom the following day.

As I talked with the mother, it was clear that she also was very depressed and was still mourning the death of her child. I arranged for the family to see a psychiatrist and the mother expressed willingness to get help because she realized the whole family was suffering. Subsequently, as I followed the family on their journey to recovery, the mother told me that she believed if I hadn't come to their house that day, she and her daughter would have committed suicide. As our paths crossed over the years, she continued to express her thanks for my help and caring. What a reward to see her return to a functioning life and to see Beth eventually go to college and step out on her own. All for taking a few moments to listen to a 12 year old who was desperately looking for someone to see that her family was suffering and needed help.

GOING HOME FOR PALLIATIVE CARE
by Joyce Brewer

Working with patients infected with HIV can be both rewarding and challenging. When that work involves pediatric patients infected with HIV, that challenge becomes even larger and more difficult emotionally. This was a job, however, that I loved. I believe I gave of myself and enabled my patients and their parents to express themselves in a non-threatening, loving, and understanding environment.

One patient in particular comes to mind. Rob was an 18-month-old who was in the last stages of AIDS. His little body was ravaged with this horrible disease. His mother was just beginning to exhibit signs of AIDS and as she watched her son dying, she was devastated. One of her biggest fears was for her son to die in the hospital. She believed very strongly that he should be able to die at home, surrounded by people who loved him. She wanted him to see his puppy, his fish, and his older brother. This was several years ago and hospice care was not available in the home for pediatric AIDS patients in our area.

I spent hours and days on the telephone with health agency representatives but neither they nor the local physicians were supportive of bringing Rob home to die. I finally located a home health agency that readily accepted this challenge. Arrangements were made. The nurse from the home health agency went to their home daily. A home pharmacy delivered IV medications to be used during his time at home. It was all set up and the day finally arrived. His mother and grandmother brought Rob home. He spent 3 days at home. He smiled for the first time in 2 months. Then he died quietly with his brother holding his hand and his puppy asleep at the foot of his bed. His mother called me and thanked me. She assured me that she finally felt at peace and wanted me to know that I made such a difference in their life. I will always remember this wonderful family.

Parish nurses get many and diverse requests from the parishioners they serve. In the next scenario, the nurse figures out a way to meet the patient's request but does it in a way that can be reversed if needed. She knew that the patient might regret her decision but rather than argue or persuade her to do it differently, she figured out a way to comply and be prepared for what she might be asked to do after the request was accomplished.

AFTER-DEATH CARE FOR THE FAMILY
by Marjorie Maddox

One of the major roles of a parish nurse is being an advocate for members of the congregation served by the church. My story is about Mr. and Mrs. D. who I worked with over a two month period of time. Mr. D. had been ill off and on for two years and had recently lapsed into a coma. During his hospitalization Mrs. D. visited every day and shared her concerns with me. She had many questions which I answered as I could. She felt intimidated by physicians and other healthcare professionals and was unable to make her concerns known to them.

Mrs. D. and I developed a close trusting relationship so when Mr. D. died I was there with her at her request. Five days after his death, she called me to talk about the cocker spaniel she had purchased four weeks earlier to keep her company. She had decided Winnie, the dog, was too much trouble so she wanted to give him away. I thought she was not ready to make this major decision so shortly after her husband's death so I contacted another member of the church and asked if she would adopt Winnie with the possibility he would not stay permanently.

Mrs. D. decided to visit her daughter out of the state for two weeks. Winnie stayed with a member of the parish and was often found sitting by the door waiting for Mrs. D. to come and get him. Mrs. D. returned one evening and by the time I got to my office I had three messages from her. She indeed missed Winnie and wanted to know if she could get Winnie back.

After a couple of phone calls I went to Mrs. D.'s house. We walked the short distance to the home where Winnie was staying. I do not know who was more excited, Mrs. D. or Winnie. As we walked home Mrs. D. constantly talked to Winnie. A follow-up phone call found both Winnie and Mrs. D. very happy.

Taking Charge to Save a Life
by Maude M. Smith

When I was a spirited 5-year-old, my beautiful RN mother had taken my 5-year-old sister and me to Nantasket Beach for an eagerly anticipated daylong outing. This was an occasion we had looked forward to with undisguised joy, for an excursion such as that was a rare treat in a middle-class family such as my own. Since we didn't have a car we traveled the 20 or so miles to the seashore by bus, an exciting adventure for any child. The other unusual happenings of that day left an indelible impression on my mind of what caring really means.

While frolicking in the sand by the edge of the sea, my sister and I noticed a couple of grown men literally dragging a third man from the turbulent breakers of a rough surf. He was a limp figure appearing half dead. Of course, we did not fully understand the seriousness of what was going on but we knew it was scary. Would-be helpers, near the rescue scene, shooed onlookers away, in order to maintain adequate space for one of the men, attempting to revive the almost lifeless swimmer. We were told by one of the rescuers only a relative would be allowed near the resuscitation effort. No relative responded. Nor did a possible companion or friend.

In a flash, my mother roughly elbowed forward through the crowd and cried out loudly, "It's all right! He is my brother!" Miraculously, it seemed, whatever she and the first rescuer did for the man worked. He slowly regained color, normal breathing, and life. My mother related these details to us later. We were kids stunned into silence and demonstrated model behavior during the actual "drama," when our mother dashed from our side to offer her help, leaving kind strangers to keep an eye on her two anxious children.

Still somewhat puzzled, at home that evening, I wondered why my mother had "lied" and so of course I asked her. She explained in simple terms that she knew she could be of assistance in a life or death situation and that in this incidence the victim was her brother."We are all sisters and brothers in this world and when necessary we must act as sisters and brothers would."

I've always remembered that day at Nantasket Beach when my mother, an RN, contributed heroically to the lifesaving efforts for a stranger, a "brother". My mother's skills and the confidence to use them from her "training school" days stood up to a crucial test.

The lessons I learned then while on an exciting pleasure trip to a favorite beach apply even now.

1. Nurses are prepared to act in emergencies and without thoughts of self. Their ethics require they use their knowledge when needed

2. We are all brothers and sisters in the "family of man".

One of the things nurses must frequently do is answer patients' questions. Most of the questions are about their health problems, but sometimes the questions are about other things such as, "Why am I dying?" or "Why is God doing this to me?" While there are no good answers for these last two questions, nurses cannot avoid a response. The nurse in the next scenario was very creative with hers.

WHEN WORDS ARE SOMETIMES ENOUGH
by Lois Plooster

Nursing is defined as the art of caring. I agree with this, but sometimes nursing breaks your heart. I was caring for a 29-year-old woman who had two children and had developed kidney failure with her last pregnancy. She was admitted for peritoneal dialysis, because her shunt was nonfunctioning. One evening, she asked me why bad things happen to people? She stated, "I have always been a good person, a good wife, and a good mother. Why has this happened to me? Why has God not healed me?"

I didn't have an answer to help her deal with life. That night at home I was watching Oh God with George Burns and he said that "God never figured out how to make good without bad, up without down, sickness without health, and life without death." I sat and thought about this and decided that I needed to remember it and something my mother always told me, "Without weeds, we would not appreciate the flowers."

So I shared this with the patient and we cried together. I will always remember her face, her sorrow, and her strength. Thank God I have had the chance to know such wonderful people in my life.

Devising ways to be innovative with physical problems happens fairly frequently, but finding approaches for solving spiritual problems is not so common. In the next scenario, the nurse uses unique ways to help a young man regain his spirit to live and move on.

CARE PLAN PRIORITIES
by April Barbara Furey Reuther

An interaction that has tugged at my heart was one that I had in my first years as a physical rehabilitation nurse. This experience defined my purpose as a "rehab" nurse.

In brief, the patient was a 22-year-old male. He had been in a horrible farm accident in which his entire right leg was mangled in a grain auger. He was depressed, suicidal, and medically unstable. Months of rehabilitation shaped his frail leg and strengthened his unsteady gait. The only aspect of care desperately needing repair was his "soul." On many of his days in rehab I gathered the staff to help me cheer him up. We watched videos, ate popcorn, and even humored him by listening to his country music. But, the best medicine was always laughter so that the end goal would be a smile.

He left and three years later, a visitor approached the nursing station on two good legs. To my surprise this was the same young man who had lived moment to moment hoping to have a pain-free, uneventful day. Now he was actually walking without assistance! It was good to realize that his goals were met and my care plan was complete three years later.

The stories in this chapter are but a few of the events that happen daily in the work of nurses. Most of the strategies that are labeled innovative or creative were not learned in school but are the inventions of nurses who feel compelled to help their patients at any expense. When barriers block their goals, when the system works against the patient, or when no one seems to care, nurses are there to see that the patient gets what's needed, what's wanted, and what's right. In many instances, the amount of innovation is directly related to the barriers that block the nurse from doing what is best for the patient.

In this day of healthcare cost containment, innovation and creativity have become more a part of the nurse's repertoire of actions. No doubt there will be more of both in the future.

REFERENCES

Oxford University Press. (1996). Oxford dictionary and thesaurus. New York: Author.

ADDITIONAL READINGS

Biddix, V. , & Brown, H. N. (1999). Establishing a parish nursing program. Nursing and Healthcare Perspectives, 20(2), 72-75.

Brennan, P. F. (1999). Harnessing innovative technologies: What can you do with a shoe? Nursing Outlook, 47(3), 128-132.

Brooten, D. , & Naylor, M. D. (1995). Nurses' effect on changing patient outcomes. Image: Journal of Nursing Scholarship, 27(2), 95-99.

Jeglin-Stoddard, A. M. & DeNatale, M. L. (1999). The challenge of change with creative collaboration. Nursing and Health Care Perspectives, 20(4), 187-193.

Manion, J. (1999). Change from within. Reflections, 25(2), 10-12.

Pierson, C. L. & Minarik, P. (1999). Professional practice: APNs in home care. American Journal of Nursing, 99(10), 22-23.

Reinhard, S. C. , Christopher, M.A. , Mason, D. J. , McConnell, K. , Rusca, P. , & Toughill, E. (1996). Promoting healthy communities through neighborhood nursing. Nursing Outlook, 44(5), 223-228.

Van Slyck, A. (1999). The stamina to succeed. Reflections, 25(2), 13-15.

CHAPTER 9

Crisis Intervention

Nurses face crises daily in many areas of practice. One of the areas most filled with crises is the emergency department (ED). The blare of the siren and the rush of feet are the sounds and movements associated with the emergency room. People responding quickly is what patients see when brought in by paramedics or who arrive because they have no other place to get care. Pain, fear, sadness, confusion, and loss are the emotions felt by patients and families who enter an emergency room. Sometimes it seems like a combat zone. Noise level high, emotions freely erupting, people to calm and patients needing a nurse NOW!

The emergency room is no place for a novice. It is not a place for the timid or the fearful. It is a place where care is quickly and efficiently provided, where teaching accompanies each case, and referrals are expertly made. Nurses working in the ER are a special breed of health care professional. They are prepared to efficiently manipulate equipment, to quickly assess and act, and to provide comfort and compassion in a calm and reassuring way. Crisis intervention is the name for this kind of nurse work.

WHY NURSES CONTINUE MAKING A DIFFERENCE
by Susan Collins

I've been a nurse for eight years and have seen and done many things. After three years in the ED you often wonder if you make any difference. People come in who are sick and dying and you stabilize them and move them.

You may sit with someone and help their family accept they are dying, while trying to keep the patient comfortable. At times it can be a frustrating job. You work hard to stabilize and intervene in someone's "crisis" and hope it helps, but never know for sure if it made a difference. Many times people return for the same thing over and over and you wonder why you even try.

On one particular night, after caring for several people who had overdosed on drugs (a few who had been there before), I went out into the waiting room and found a young man in his early 20s who was clean and well-dressed. He said, "I took a whole bottle of Tylenol." While I helped him get into bed and obtained his medical history, I asked if he had ever tried this before. To my surprise, he said, "No." I proceeded with his history and learned he had cancer of the bone, was finishing college, and was from a good, supportive family. He said everything was getting to him and he was pretty upset. I told him because of the Tylenol and his medical history, we would have to run some tests and would have to wash out his stomach. I explained the procedure would make him vomit. I also told him it would go a lot better if he cooperated. He tolerated everything as well as could be expected. He remained stable and even joked about the smell of the medicine I was giving him to counteract his high Tylenol levels.

On the way to the Intensive Care Unit, I explained to him we would send people in to talk to him and I hoped he would accept their help. I also told him I hoped I wouldn't see him again unless he was coming in to bring us some pizza.

Several months passed and one evening I was asked to go to the front desk. I went out and noticed this young man. When I asked what was wrong, he said, "I didn't know what kind of pizza to bring, so I brought cheese. Thanks for everything you did that night." As he turned to leave, I realized that in the few hours I had spent with him I had made a difference in his life and I knew he was going to be okay. I don't think I did anything special. I do my job every day to the best of my abilities. As frustrating and hard as it is to jump in and out of people's lives, I enjoy what I do. Every once in awhile I can take pride in the fact that, because of my interventions, someone's life was made a little better.

The nurse stories in this chapter are a sample of the many stories nurses could tell about helping people in crisis. They illustrate the variety of crises that the nurse must be able to respond to and the depth of knowledge and skill the nurse must have. They also demonstrate the impact patients make on nurses and how nurses cope with death and life-threatening events day after day.

FINELY HONED NURSING SKILLS
by Gary Laustsen

It was still early into the beginning of another night shift when the child arrived at the triage area of our community hospital's ER. He was being carried by his father. The Mother was hovering close by. The parents were very anxious and the child was listless and lethargic. They were from Vietnam and their English was minimal adding to our difficulty in finding out what was going on. The child was moved immediately to our critical care room.

The 4-year old had been sick for the past 4 days with vomiting, diarrhea, and fever. The parents had tried to treat their son as best they could. However, the child continued to get worse. He was more lethargic, pale, non-responsive, and flaccid. I immediately called the ER physician and started setting up for an IV. Starting an IV is a routine I've done a thousand times, and it sometimes seems the basic nursing skills we do every day are just practice for the one time it will really make a difference. As the physician entered the room he recognized the severity of this child's condition and after my first attempt at inserting an IV failed, he tried to find access. Two attempts and two punctures left us still without IV access. I can remember the intense focus I had as I looked at the hand of the child and knew I could "get a line in." A few moments later and we were pushing fluid through the IV tubing in the child's hand and breathing a big sigh of relief that we could now revive the child.

Soon, the pediatrician on-call arrived and arranged for transport of the child to the children's hospital in a nearby city where I also worked part-time in the ER. By calling to their ICU later that night, I learned the child was doing fine. I can't say if the IV I started saved the child's life, but I do know it made a difference.

Sometimes, no matter the skill and quality of the interventions, lives are lost. Many times, other lives can be saved from these losses, as in the following stories.

HIGHER INTERVENTIONS
by Shirley White

The most memorable experience in my nursing career is what happened when my son Jef died. He was killed in a truck accident in the rural northeast corner of Iowa. The area was served by a volunteer ambulance crew, which probably took at least half an hour to respond if not longer. Luckily, a nurse whom I had formerly worked with happened to be driving by and stopped to help.

She did not know who Jef was at the time because she hadn't seen him in 15 years, but she immediately began CPR and continued until the ambulance arrived. Jef was taken to the local hospital where he was stabilized and then flown to a trauma center, 60 miles away. At the time, I was home by myself with no way to contact my husband and my other son. I only remember feeling panicked about what to do, so I sat down and said a prayer. Then I'm sure God and my nursing background took over.

I called the ED physician caring for Jef. He told me Jef was very unstable and they would be doing brain studies. I knew from what he told me that Jef was no longer with us.

A little history will help with this story. Jef's cousin had lost his kidneys from a rare disease a year or so previously. Jef had offered immediately to donate one of his kidneys since the two cousins were like brothers. Jef was tested in May just before coming home on vacation and was almost a perfect match, closer than members of his cousin's immediate family. Jef had helped with a fund-raiser for his cousin. On Friday, June 16, his cousin was put on the National Donor List because the doctors wanted to try for a cadaver kidney before using Jef's kidney. Jef's accident happened the next day on Saturday.

The very next evening, my other son sat at the bedside before and after his cousin's transplant. I will never forget him telling me how much more at peace he felt, watching his cousin get better each hour after the surgery his brother made possible.

At Jef's funeral, the nurse who stopped to help at the accident scene came to me crying because she felt she had let me down. But it was her caring and skills, as well as those of the volunteers on the ambulance team, that made it possible for Jef to fulfill his wish to help his cousin and others with organ donations. Otherwise, he would have just been another motor vehicle statistic, dying in the backwoods of northeast Iowa.

Beyond the robotic protocols that save lives, ED nurses are compassionate and caring practitioners. They balance efficiency with tenderness. The nurse in the next story had a tough decision to make, and chose to stay with the patient even though he was criticized for doing so. His display of compassion, commitment, and tenderness clearly set him apart as a nurse who cares.

NOT LETTING THEM DIE ALONE
by John P. Lussier

I was working as a staff nurse when an elderly man was brought in by ambulance. His neighbor accompanied him but did not stay long. The patient knew he would die, but he did not want to come to the hospital. The neighbor, however, did not want the responsibility of being around when he died. In fact, she left shortly after getting him to the hospital.

We put him in one of our three cardiac bays and watched and waited. No one was really assigned to him, but I kept checking on his status as I attended to other patients. As his death drew near, I checked on him more frequently. At one point, the physician suggested I might use my time better if I spent more time with the living patients and less with a dying one.

I spoke to my charge nurse and she took over the rest of my patient load so that I could be with him. I didn't think anyone should die alone, so I just sat there with him until he died. Then I took a few minutes to make the transition from that situation to facing living patients and then relieved my charge nurse of my patient load. I'm proud I chose to stay with the patient and I hope someone will be there for me when I die so I won't be alone.

Most nurses have cared for people in crisis who are hostile, combative, uncooperative, confused, or belligerent because they are anxious, scared or under the influence of alcohol or drugs. In these instances, like others, nurses make every effort to provide quality care, which includes compassion and sensitive treatment. The next story is an excellent example of how compassionate care can make a difference, a difference the nurse may never know about. Fortunately, in this case, the nurse did learn how her tenderness and sensitive care affected the patient.

MAKING TIME COUNT
by Iris Davis

After being an ER nurse for 23 years, I've come to realize I don't always know what my patients really need. How arrogant of me to have ever thought I could understand what is best for these people I care for after spending only a few minutes with them. I don't know what they have gone through that has shaped them into the person I see on a stretcher in my emergency department. I try very hard to remember this especially with those "difficult" patients who show up in emergency rooms.

One day I had "Larry" as a patient. He was an alcoholic in his early 40s. His kind and gentle dad was with him this day, and was trying to keep Larry from becoming too rude. It wasn't working. All of us in the ER and the local police department know Larry. Sometimes he can be pretty mean, and today was no exception. He was impatient ping-ponging between rudeness and profuse apologies, and smelled like his last bath had been in Jack Daniels.

The ER was busy, but I was trying hard to remember to convey compassion during every procedure I could in every way I could. Larry gave me a wonderful opportunity to practice. He was obstinate. He took forever to comply with requests. He was impatient. He didn't want to listen to his discharge instructions. I kept trying. I knew I wasn't going to make any dramatic changes in Larry's life, but I felt there was something I needed to say or do. I just had no clue what was needed. As I helped Larry get out of the wheel chair to get into his dad's car, I did what a lot of us nurses do when protocols don't apply, or pathways desert us. I went on gut instinct. I put my hand lightly on Larry's shoulder and quietly said, "God bless you Larry. Now you take care of yourself!" Larry mumbled something, but avoided eye contact as he lurched into the car. As I rolled the wheelchair back to the ER, I wondered why I said what I did, and if anything could make any difference to Larry. Did I actually help him, or was I just deluding myself?

A week went by, maybe two. A clerk came up to me and told me a man was looking for me. I didn't recognize Larry. He was clean. He was sober. He walked up to me like a little kid and said, "I wanted to say thank you for taking care of me. I wanted to give you something." At first I was really uncomfortable. I don't accept gifts from patients. But what made me more uncomfortable was that Larry looked and acted so completely different than the way I had come to know him! It's a little scary when people you think you know act in an uncharacteristic fashion even if the change is for the better. Then I looked at his face, and I saw that he had a need to thank me. I told him I appreciated his thanks, but he didn't have to give me anything. Larry disagreed and said, "It's not much, but I'd like you to have it." He handed me a roll of lifesaver candies. I said, "Thank you," and felt myself get a little teary eyed. Larry walked away, and I held onto the candy. I think perhaps the lesson Larry taught me was as valuable to me as my attempts of patience and compassion were to him.

I didn't do anything dramatic. I didn't say anything all that profound or wise. I didn't save or change Larry's life. I didn't take any extra time, I just made good use of the time I had. It seems like such a small thing that I did, but if I can just keep trying to do the small things well, perhaps that's the best I can hope for. Like throwing a pebble into still water, I'll never know what the long-term ripple effects will be. As a staff nurse, I'm going to keep trying to do my best and care for my patients even when they aren't easy to care for. I believe the ones who are hardest to love are the ones who need love the most.

Patient teaching is a vital strategy in all crises. However, timing of the teaching is important. In the next scenario, the nurse discovers just how important timing can be in alleviating patient anxiety.

PATIENT TEACHING AS CRISIS INTERVENTION
by Gary Sanders

I was working the night shift last April. The night had been going fairly well. The majority of the patients we saw were treated and released. At around 5 a.m. an ambulance crew called. They were bringing us a 50-year-old male complaining of chest pain.

The patient, Mr. K., arrived and after placing him on our cardiac monitor and doing an EKG, we noted he was having a heart attack. Mr. K. was told of his condition and I saw the look of fear and apprehension on his face. The doctor explained we would give a medicine, called TPA, intravenously to relieve the blockage.

I stayed with him throughout the procedure and tried to talk to him and asked if he understood what was happening, but he never spoke a word. Mr. K.'s wife was with him and she, too, looked very fearful and even cried for a bit along with Mr. K. I explained what would happen but it fell on deaf ears. Both of them were in a state of shock.

I transferred Mr. K. to the cardiac care unit at around 6:30 a.m. and told him I would come see him before I left the hospital that morning. He spoke for the first time, "That would be nice." I left and returned to my unit.

When I got back to his room just after 7 a.m. he did not look so frightened anymore. I sat in a chair and he asked, "When will the danger be over." I looked at him with a puzzled look. Then his wife said, "The doctor told us there were great risks involved in getting TPA (a clot buster)." So, I sat with Mr. K. and his wife and explained what the risks were and that most had passed. I also described the catherterization procedure so he would be prepared for the experience. I left his room after a while and he actually had a bit of a smile on his face. He and his wife thanked me for all the hard work we had done in the ED.

I visited Mr. K. often. Each time he told me about his catheterization and how well it went. I watched him get better and leave the hospital. We still keep in touch by phone about once a month and he is doing well. He and his wife tell me how wonderful the staff was at the hospital and how much they appreciated my helping them understand what was happening when he was so scared.

One form of patient teaching is by example. While this next scenario is not a common one, it illustrates how powerful and compelling teaching by example can be. The nurse in this story helps the patient cope by using her own similar experience as an example. The patient learns much about her therapy and the nurse learns more about her own ability to cope.

HAVING EXPERIENCE WITH THE PATIENT'S SITUATION
by M. Heckendorn

I have breast cancer. I am in the midst of chemotherapy and just past all the surgical interventions. I am thankful for a future, but I am frightened of what may be ahead. I am happy to have treatments available to me, but I am angry that I have to endure them.

I have recently returned to work in the ED. On that first day, I picked up a patient's chart, noting orders for an IV, lab work, and medication for pain and vomiting. I gathered the supplies and prepared to go into the patient's room. On my way in, I read the history of the patient and learned she had breast cancer with metastasis, and was 47 years old, 3 years younger than me. I stopped dead in my tracks. I couldn't go into that room but I heard the patient retching and the department was terribly busy. I also knew she would have to wait longer for her treatments if I didn't do them. I didn't think I could face it.

She was pale, shivering, and huddled in a ball. I called her name and said I was there to help her. Her husband sat silently in the corner. She said, "I am so sick. I am not ready for this. I told them I was too sick for chemotherapy." She began to cry and breathe rapidly. "My breathing gets bad when I get scared," she said. I touched her shoulder and told her we would give her medications to lessen her pain and nausea. I asked her about her chemotherapy. She hadn't had any yet, but had an infusaport in place. I told her we would use it to give her the medication.

She became hysterical. Her port had never been used. She didn't know what to expect. She said she couldn't do this. My moment had arrived. It was time for me to confront my disease. I told her I also had breast cancer and had the same type of port. I hugged her hard and said I knew she could do this. I told her that breast cancer patients are survivors. She became calm and began to ask questions.

We started an IV, gave her medication, and took x-rays. Her pain lessened and her nausea subsided. She was able to walk. I tucked her into a wheelchair and got her ready to go to an inpatient room. She smiled, made a joke, and thanked me. I cried all the way home that night. I cried for every woman who has this disease. I cried for my worst fears for myself. I cried for her. I cried that I had doubted myself.

A major aspect of caring for persons in crisis is being able to quickly obtain the information necessary for making an accurate diagnosis and establishing a therapeutic plan. Gathering information from persons who are in crisis takes someone who is a skillful communicator, someone who can ask the right questions and listen for the overt and subtle responses. The next scenario is an excellent example of how therapeutic communication—as a crisis intervention—is a valuable and necessary tool for gathering the needed data.

CARING FOR THE WHOLE PATIENT
Melissa Blevins Jones

I graduated from nursing school and went to work on the second shift in the second busiest emergency department in the Commonwealth of Virginia. I had been working for 6 months when I walked into the room of a patient I'll call Robert, who was being seen for symptoms of dehydration. After I performed the initial assessment, the doctor saw him. While I was starting his I.V., we began to talk about his life and his illness. He was HIV positive and had the AIDS virus. While I worked, I asked him questions about support systems available and how he was doing emotionally and spiritually.

He responded like a floodgate had opened. He talked about how difficult it was to watch his lover die, how he had enjoyed traveling around the United States and abroad, how successful he was in this job and how wounded he felt when he had to leave. We talked about the misconceptions people have about HIV. He told me how his family had been so supportive of him, and how it was humbling for him to have to move back into his parent's home at the age of 37. We talked about death and he said something I will never forget. He said, "Death is not the enemy, suffering is the enemy."

After he received his IV fluids and medication, he was discharged. Before he left, I gave him a big hug and I said, "Take care of you, OK?" He promised he would and left. About 6 weeks later, I received a package at work. It was a handmade booklet and it read: "To love, you must be loved. Thanks for being all you are. And caring for all of me! Love, Robert"

On the final page were six pictures of him in various settings and costumes, and beside them, he wrote, "Yes, they all are me". That handmade booklet filled me up with, "feel good." I cannot adequately express in written words how much Robert's handmade booklet meant to me. He was thanking me for addressing not only his physical needs, but also his emotional and spiritual needs. I have never been so proud to be a nurse!

In order for nurses to be effective in crises they must be able to cope with the environment and the needs of the patients. They must be able to help the patient and remain calm, compassionate, and skillful. Some nurses use faith and prayer while others use each other for support.

EMERGENCY NURSING
by Mary Mesikapp

The door of our ambulance popped open with a rush of hot air. With adrenaline pumping, all eyes scanned a short, brown-haired young man. His skin was pale as the sheet he rested beneath. With two intravenous lines, his body was immobilized on a long board with his neck in a stiff uncomfortable collar. There also was a cardiac monitor and oxygen in place.

This young teen, while riding his bicycle home, collided with a truck and was severely injured. He was barely conscious as the medics rushed him into trauma room #1. I managed to fight my way to the head of the bed, searching for his face beneath the bandages.

"Hello, what's your name?" I quickly asked. "Jim," he said eyes focused but wildly searching the room, "I'm scared," he shouted, "What's going on? Am I going to die?" "Please look at me," I encouraged, "There are many people here to do many things. We are all here to help you. Look at my eyes. My name is Mary, I'm with you. I'll be here, talk to me," I said as my team members frantically worked to keep him stable. Then I scanned his body, head to toe, for my 60-second assessment. I was scared for Jim. What I noted was not good at all. Just proximal to his left groin was a fast growing hematoma, his respirations were fast, and it looked like he had fractured ribs on his left side. His skin was still pale. High-flow oxygen continued to blow into his nose and mouth but who knew how much it was helping. Vital signs on arrival were somewhat stable. I talked as calmly as I could, reassuring Jim. He pleaded with his eyes to stop all the pain. I moved to his side, held his trembling hand and said a silent prayer, "Please God, help us help him. He's so young. Lord, help us."

We talked briefly about his parents. He told me to tell them he didn't mean to get in trouble, and that he loved them. I squeezed his cold, pale hand and noticed dusky nail beds. I hoped to give him my strength. It was hard to believe it was only a few minutes since his arrival and we were ready for surgery. "Dear Lord, please be with him. Lead him to you if it is his time. Give him peace," I prayed as I saw his pupils dilate and vital signs plummet to minimal.

His face grew still. We rushed him to surgery with six intravenous lines in place for fluid, resuscitation, and blood products. As the OR and trauma staff rushed him down the hall, a pool of blood trailed behind. After Jim was in their hands, I found a blood-soaked driver's permit in the back pocket of his shredded jeans. As I struggled to identify his full name, address, and phone number, I rushed the information to our Chaplain. Then I pulled the curtain to close out the chaotic, noisy environment and cried for Jim, his family and his friends. But I also thanked Jim because he reminded me I became an Emergency Department (ED) nurse because I wanted to make a difference in people's lives one person at a time. I will never forget the lesson of Jim. I will always remember he was someone's family. He deserved respect and compassionate tender loving care.

Death is a common event in the ED and, like everyone else, nurses feel the loss. While they provide support and comfort for the family and prepare the dead patient for organ transplant, they grieve. When a child dies it is even harder for the nurse. Each nurse has an individual way of coping, and the next story, told by an ED nurse, demonstrates her power of faith when coping with the death of a child.

Finding a Reason Behind the Tragedy
by Julie A. Louder

The most impressionable experience that I still recall as vividly as if it just happened involved a little 3-year old girl. This sweet child had been playing outside on a pleasant spring evening. Her mother was attempting to shoot a rabbit that had wandered into their garden. She dropped the shotgun firing a bullet that lodged in the child's head, right above her eye. One of my best friends, a wonderful nurse, happened to be riding along with the ambulance unit that responded to the emergency call.

This incident occurred in a mountainous area. A rather long trip became even longer with each dismal medic report that was received. A pediatric code was designated and the trauma team was in place when the ambulance arrived. My supervisor became my team member as we assumed care of this child. Each of us were mothers, and I am sure we pushed all thoughts of our own children to the far corners of our minds, attempting to keep emotions at bay so we could keep focused on providing care for the child. I cannot recall all the clinical specifics of this incident but we did obtain an EEG and a head CT. All medical and drug interventions had been accomplished and it was evident that despite all medical technology, this sweet child was going to die.

The one memory that still haunts me is hearing this child's mother in the hallway outside the room screaming, "Oh dear God, I've shot my baby!" Suddenly I started to cry. The tears fell on my trauma gown and mixed with the child's blood. I did not try to hide my tears. I could not leave the side of this little one. Finally the heart-wrenching decision was made by the parents that their daughter's organs would be donated. The transplant team was en route and although I knew that nothing we would do now would matter, I stayed at the child's side. I wiped her face and dressed her in a bright-colored pediatric gown. A short while later she was transferred to the hospital critical care unit to wait for the transplant team.

Ten years and many experiences later, this beautiful little girl's life and death is still a part of me. Although I do not fully understand why it happened, I believe that God has a purpose in everything, and allows things to happen for a reason. Before this night, I did not know this child. I believe she came into my life for a reason, and God entrusted her to my care. Now, I know why I am a nurse.

Caring for patients in crisis is not limited to emergency rooms in urban and rural hospitals. It occurs in many settings and all around the globe. The next story, about a nurse in Bosnia, demonstrates how nurses help each other cope with crisis.

WHEN THE WAR FRONTLINE IS YOUR HOMETOWN
by Music Marina

This story is about a nurse and war in Bosnia. One day in 1993, I was out with my friends. We heard on the radio that all nurses were to return to the hospital. So I did. When I arrived I saw many injured people. One lady had been wounded in her right leg, left arm, and abdomen. She was calling for her sons. In a minute, my hands were covered with her blood. I told myself I needed to start an infusion and stop the bleeding. She took my hand and asked me about her sons and I could only answer, "I don't know."

While I was alone with that woman in the emergency room, there was an admission of two boys about two years old. I went out front to see them. Both of the little boys had been decapitated. I still can hear the crying of that mother as she called out to her dead sons.

My next patients were two of my friends. One had a head injury and needed mechanical ventilation. The other was dead. We grew up together on the same street and now she was gone forever. I had no time to grieve because another patient needed my help. I was working and crying. My heart was breaking. I knew I had to do my work and keep the next patient alive until surgery. Each minute seemed like a year, but we did get him to the operating room. I don't know the number of injured people we cared for that day.

I remember when I sat down with the rest of the nurses in the emergency room of the hospital we talked about the fact that there are no rules in war. Death doesn't discriminate if you're a child, woman, man, mother, or someone's sister.

The nurses in Bosnia work every day to help and provide better kinds of treatment. The greatest reward we can get is when patients return to say "thank you for the help." Nursing around here means to be a friend or to offer a helping hand to a mother or little child. It means a lot and I am proud to say I am a nurse in Bosnia.

Nursing means a great deal, not only to those who practice it, but also to those patients whose stories are told in this book. As the stories in this book indicate, to intervene in a crisis takes considerable knowledge and skill, and varies depending on the persons involved and the type of crisis. However, there is one aspect of a crisis, and the way that nurses respond, that must not be overlooked and which is clearly evident in each story presented. Crisis intervention as a therapeutic strategy is strongly humanistic, that is, the intervention is based on the belief that people are valuable and worth special attention (Kosier, Erb, & Blais, 1997). During the acute phase of a crisis, which the stories in this chapter addressed, it is the role of the nurse to restore the person to the pre-trauma level of functioning. Once the crisis is over, the nurse can help the individual develop adaptive behaviors to move on or, if the crisis brought death, the nurse makes sure it occurs with dignity. Sustaining is the key and, clearly, the nurses in this chapter sustained.

REFERENCES

Cowen, P. S. (1998). Crisis child care: An intervention for at-risk families. Issues in Comprehensive Pediatric Nursing, 21(3), 147-158.

Kozier, B., Erb, G., & Blais, K. (1997). (3rd Ed.). Professional nursing practice: Concept and perspectives. Men Lo Park, CA: Addison-Wesley.

Osterman, J. E., & Chemtob, C. M. (1999). Emergency intervention for acute traumatic stress. Psychiatric Services, 50(6), 739-40.

Ratna, L. (1998). Crisis intervention: The Barnet expereince. Alternative Health International, 1(1), 1-9.

Reisch, T., Schlatter, P., & Tschaher, W. (19??). Efficacy of crisis intervention. Crisis, 20(2), 78-85.

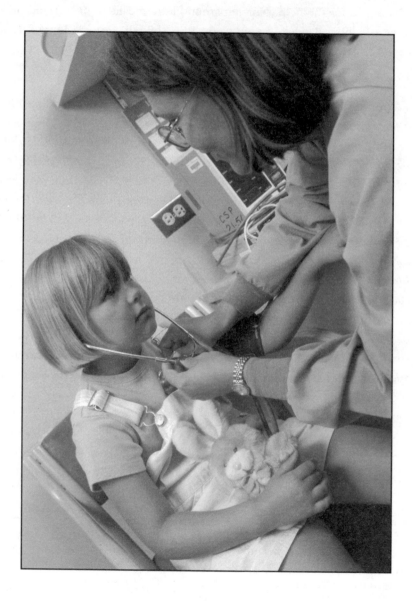

CHAPTER 10

Conclusion

A book about nurse work is difficult to complete because there are so many stories about what nurses do and so many ways to tell the world about nurses' contributions in the lives of people. It seems fitting, then, to end this book with three stories that clearly demonstrate the impact nurses make and how sometimes it is merely their presence that "makes the difference."

NURSING PEERS
Susan Mazzenga

I had just completed a routine day at work. The headache that had been present all week, wasn't any worse, until I bent over to pick up my purse! It felt like I had been hit in the head with an ax. The pain was excruciating! I held onto the sink edge to remain on my feet. The feeling finally subsided some and I could stand upright but my legs felt funny. I, being a nurse, of course ignored it and kept going to my car. The whole time I was walking I could feel "pins and needles" progressing up my body. I reached the car and realized I had to go back. The short distance I walked back to the hospital seemed like miles and by the time I got there my hands were like claws and I had no control over them. Fear was quickly settling in. I got into the ER where Suzanne, quickly put me into a chair and tried to get some sort of history as to the prior events.

She saw that I was deteriorating quickly and tried to get me to a stretcher. I started to collapse and had trouble breathing. She immediately called for help while reassuring me. Two IV lines were inserted and nasal oxygen and monitor leads were put on me in record time. All the time, Suzanne was telling me what was being done and reassuring me. Blood was drawn for analysis. By now I was in a total panic and totally aphasic. All I could do was make incoherent moans. Suzanne held me close and comforted me while calmly calling out what had to be done. She accompanied me to the CT Scanner so I would not be alone.

The worse part of this ordeal was that I was totally alert and oriented. Suzanne never left my side through it all and reassured and comforted me constantly. Suzanne and my doctor were forced to give me a tissue plasminogen activator (TPA, a clot buster) where I was or risk missing the window of opportunity for maximum effectiveness. I was given the TPA and transferred to a larger hospital.

I was "in" and "out," but every time I opened my eyes Suzanne was there holding my hand and giving me reassurances. She got permission to ride with me in the ambulance, even though it wasn't necessary and stayed with me until things were to her satisfaction. My coworkers, the doctors and other staff members, saved my life, but I would never have made it back if it hadn't been for Suzanne, an RN who was "always there."

The next story is also about "being there," but it illustrates how nurses do not always know about their impact until later. Some nurses never know what a few moments, or a few words, do for people. In this case, the student nurse learned an important lesson, one that is not usually described in a textbook.

TEACHING MOMENTS
by Donna A. Redding

One of my senior nursing students cared for a retired nurse 2 weeks ago who had been diagnosed with colon cancer. This brave woman had been diagnosed only a few days prior to this, and had made the decision to receive no treatment. I visited with her one morning, and we began to talk about her decision. She became a little teary but said "You know what treatment is like. I don't ever want to die like that." I supported the fact that her decision was hers alone and we would provide her with the care and comfort she needed.

She then diverted her attention to my student as the student was asking about the patient's lower leg edema. The patient turned to me and said, "It's time to teach, instructor!" I discussed the development of edema with the student at the patient's bedside, including her in the discussion. During our assessment, I identified a warm red spot on her lower extremity. She then started teaching, quizzing the student about inflammation and the possible cause of the spot. She helped the student identify a possible deep vein clot, and the two of us encouraged and cheered the student on as she contacted the patient's physician to initiate vein studies, heparin therapy, and bed rest orders.

This patient told me of the importance and how she wished she could talk with me all day "because we have so many stories to share." She commended me on my assessment, teaching, and critical thinking skills. I, in turn, commended her on hers, and thanked her for her input into my student's learning experience. She indicated that she had never been an instructor, but had always wanted to be. She said, "You have lots more important things to do than to stand here and talk to an old gal like me." I told her that spending time with her was exactly what I needed to be doing at that moment. When it was time to leave, she encouraged me to return. Unfortunately, I didn't have the chance.

Although this woman appeared quite stable when my student and I cared for her, she died the following week. We never heard the exact cause of her death but I was honored and humbled at the fact that my student and I had a small part in her comfort.

Overall, I was able to provide her with caring, active listening, attentive assessment, facilitation of appropriate treatment, and the opportunity to serve as an instructor. I will remember this great nurse for a very long time.

The final story of this book was selected because it demonstrates the real power nurses have: the power to influence the thinking and coping abilities of others. By providing information, sharing experiences, and giving of self, the nurse made a lasting difference in the lives of the patient and his daughter. This happens daily and in every area of the world.

What would we do without nurses?

Everyday Acts of Kindness
by Sandra Strobel

I was on my way to a quick lunch already tasting the wonderful soup of the day, when I rounded the corner and nearly stepped on a crumpled human, slouched in a heap on the floor just outside the ICU doors. I immediately recognized Opal, the daughter of one of our very ill patients who had been taken to surgery that morning. I knelt beside her and took her into my arms. She pulled me tight against her in desperate need. Her whimpers became bellows of sobbing. Knowing whatever consumed her was far too painful to explain, I just sat holding her. No one was around. It was as if God cleared the area for a sanctuary of quietness for her to grieve.

After a long interval, she quieted to a soft sighing, then slowly lifted her head to see who was holding her. When she saw me through her tears, she could only whimper, "Thank you," before a flood of emotions overtook her again. Finally, she said that the doctors had just told the family that "Daddy would likely not make it out of surgery this time." His extensive burns had kept him in critical condition and after a long fight, he was losing the battle.

My compassion was intensified as memories of losing my own father only a year before came back. As I cried with her, I was able to tell her honestly I knew how she felt. I had been there, done that. Not all nursing interactions have that element of experience within them. Somehow, hearing I had recently traveled that road, she was comforted. "How does it feel to lose your dad who was your best friend?" she intently inquired.

In that 30-minute lunch break, I was able to comfort her and say how God gives you the strength to accept a father's absence, even though you miss him. My father's death had just served a purpose.

By the time I had to return to work, Opal was composed and feeling stronger. But I pondered that event the rest of the day. I hadn't eaten or relaxed, but somehow I was energized by that interaction of caring that had been arranged for me. I knew it was not a coincidence but a divine assignment to offer caring to a desperate soul. I was the one chosen to come to her in her need. And she had been touched and lifted.

I left my job soon after that to attend graduate school and did not hear about her until nearly 4 years later, when I was with a group caroling for hospitalized patients just before Christmas. As we strolled the halls of a surgical unit, a young lady approached me, "Do you remember me?" she asked. "I was the one you rescued in the halls of ICU when my dad was burned so badly." I did remember her. She told me her father was here having some minor plastic surgery repair, and she wanted me to see him.

"So you are the one who prayed us through the dark days?" he said. He was bright and alert, scarred, but delightful. "You are among the special people who helped us through those tough times."

"Sir, I never got to see you awake," I spoke in amazement at the miracle before me. "You were unconscious the entire time I worked ICU. It is a pleasure to know the person who came back to life after such a long time in critical condition." Our time together was brief but touching. His recovery was nothing short of a miracle. I was acutely reminded of the effects of reaching out beyond the duties of a job description.

And so it is with all we do as nurses, as people who care. It may be as simple as a smile, as long as a lunch break, or a deed unnoticed. We may never know what each act of kindness does for others. As our lives pass theirs, it is always wise to reach out. Be careful when you entertain strangers, for in so doing, "some have entertained angels unawares" (Hebrews 13:2).

Summary

The nurses who provided the stories for this book are often reluctant to be acknowledged as important practitioners who make a difference in the lives of many people. Clearly, their contributions have been incredible and substantial, but much of what they do is invisible and, thus, under-valued.

The purpose for writing this book and sharing these nurse stories is to showcase the nurse as a competent and courageous healthcare provider who uses critical thinking, crisis intervention and creativity to care and comfort patients in a variety of settings. They do nurse work and do it skillfully and unselfishly with little praise or compensation. There are not enough books written or television shows and movies produced to demonstrate their worth. It is the author's hope that this book will provide the reader with a new and enlightened awareness of the person who cared enough to make a difference when people needed it most.

Books Published by the Honor Society of Nursing, Sigma Theta Tau International

A Daybook for Nurses: Making a Difference Each Day, Hudacek, 2004.

The Adventurous Years: Leaders in Action 1973-1999, Henderson, 1998.

As We See Ourselves: Jewish Women in Nursing, Benson, 2001.

Building and Managing a Career in Nursing: Strategies for Advancing Your Career, Miller, 2003.

Cadet Nurse Stories: The Call for and Response of Women During World War II, Perry and Robinson, 2001.

Collaboration for the Promotion of Nursing, Briggs, Merk, and Mitchell, 2003.

Creating Responsive Solutions to Healthcare Change, McCullough, 2001.

Gerontological Nursing Issues for the 21st Century, Gueldner and Poon, 1999.

The HeART of Nursing: Expressions of Creative Art in Nursing, Wendler, 2002.

The Image Editors: Mind, Spirit, and Voice, Hamilton, 1997.

Immigrant Women and Their Health: An Olive Paper, Ibrahim Meleis, Lipson, Muecke and Smith, 1998.

The Language of Nursing Theory and Metatheory, King and Fawcett, 1997.

Making a Difference: Stories from the Point of Care, Volume I, Hudacek, 2005.

Making a Difference: Stories from the Point of Care, Volume II, Hudacek, 2004.

The Neuman Systems Model and Nursing Education: Teaching Strategies and Outcomes, Lowry, 1998.

Nurses' Moral Practice: Investing and Discounting Self, Kelly, 2000.

Nursing and Philanthropy: An Energizing Metaphor for the 21st Century, McBride, 2000.

Ordinary People, Extraordinary Lives: The Stories of Nurses, Smeltzer and Vlasses, 2003.

Pivotal Moments in Nursing: Leaders Who Changed the Path of a Profession, Houser and Player, 2004.

Roy Adaptation Model-Based Research: 25 Years of Contributions to Nursing Science, Boston Based Adaptation Research in Nursing Society, 1999.

Stories of Family Caregiving: Reconsideration of Theory, Literature, and Life, Poirier and Ayres, 2002.

Virginia Avenel Henderson: Signature for Nursing, Hermann, 1997.

For more information and to order these books from the Honor Society of Nursing, Sigma Theta Tau International, visit the society's Web site at **www.nursingsociety. org/publications,** or go to **www.nursingknowledge.org/stti/books,** the Web site of Nursing Knowledge International, the honor society's sales and distribution division, or call 1.888.NKI.4.YOU (U.S. and Canada) or +1.317.634.8171 (Outside U.S. and Canada).